CON

M000013557

INTRODUCTION

"Jesus called them over and said, 'You know that the ones who are considered the rulers by the Gentiles show off their authority over them and their high-ranking officials order them around. But that's not the way it will be with you. Whoever wants to be great among you will be your servant. Whoever wants to be first among you will be the slave of all, for the Human One didn't come to be served but rather to serve and to give his life to liberate many people.'"

Mark 10:42-45, CEB

This journal is for you—leaders of the church. Our hope is that, over a three-month period, you take time to intentionally reflect and cast your vision to lead God's people, embody God's grace, and offer ministry in God's name for the church and the world. This journal offers relevant scripture passages, inspirational stories, insightful information, expert advice, and space for journaling. The commitment of the General Board of Higher Education and Ministry is to journey with you as together we nurture leaders and change lives. It is our hope that as you lead with integrity and authenticity, you continue to discover, claim, and flourish in your leadership context.

DISCOVER

1
DISCOVER YOUR LEADERSHIP

"I know the plans I have in mind for you, declares the LORD; they are plans for peace, not disaster, to give you a future filled with hope."

Jeremiah 29:11, CEB

Leaders see the vision, the people, the resources, and the mission. Likewise, leaders are called to cultivate and nurture team members and help them discover, claim, and flourish in their own leadership skills. Consequently, leadership is a generative process in which leaders beget leaders and, in the case of Christian leaders, help usher in God's reign. Discovery is the process by which leaders help their team optimize their capabilities and gifts. It is a progressive plan built both on the group and individual level. For the group, leaders lay out a plan to shape the group's leadership. The group members then can act as catalysts for each other, thereby creating a bonded team of trusted peers who aspire to help each other reach their potential. As individuals, they also require a plan for their personal development based on their own capabilities and potential. This means that they need to commit and challenge themselves in order to strengthen their weaknesses and optimize their gifts. The leader helps by tracking progress and giving feedback, remembering that each person has a unique style of leadership that needs to be developed.

PRAYER

Holy God, I know you have a plan for each of us. Help me be open to your leading.

What can you do to help your team
discover their leadership?

—2—
CLAIM YOUR LEADERSHIP

"Let your roots grow down into him, and let your lives be
built on him. Then your faith will grow strong
in the truth you were taught, and you will
overflow with thankfulness."

Colossians 2:7, NLT

Like a deeply rooted tree, some people have solid character, values, experiences, and fortitude. At first glance, others may appear resilient on the surface, but when a crisis or challenge comes their way, they fold and become indecisive or even quit. Their roots can't or won't hold. Like discovery, claiming and living into one's leadership role is an ongoing project. As leaders, we want to ensure that every team member can handle adversity and make tough decisions as they lay claim to their own leadership. We need to find ways to deepen their values, commitments, and understanding. We need to deepen their self-awareness as well as our own. It's not just about the skill to perform but the interpersonal context in which leadership is relevant.

PRAYER

Dear God, deepen my sense of purpose and grant me the wisdom to serve those I lead.

How do you lay claim to your authority and leadership?

3

FLOURISH IN LEADERSHIP

"Trust in the LORD with all your heart; don't rely
on your own intelligence. Know him in all your paths,
and he will keep your ways straight."

Proverbs 3:5-6, CEB

Everyone wants to flourish. To meet this need, people need direction and guidance about taking the right path. Without direction, they can become lost and lose heart. A leader's responsibility is to give people both the truth and consequences. This means giving a clear understanding of what success looks like, what constitutes the best choices, and insight to where and why you are leading in a particular direction. Leaders need to give parameters, offer advice, and instill confidence. Likewise, in order to flourish, people want to know leaders will be there for them when and if they are needed. Everyone has dreams, and it is up to leaders to help bring these aspirations to life in light of the mission and common goals.

PRAYER

Dear God, I'll try my best today, but if I lose my hope, please remind me that your plans are better than my dreams.

What do you need right now in order
to flourish in your leadership?

4

DISCOVER ALL THE PEOPLE

"Now Deborah, a prophet, the wife of Lappidoth, was a leader of Israel at that time. She would sit under Deborah's palm tree between Ramah and Bethel in the Ephraim highlands, and the Israelites would come to her to settle disputes."

Judges 4:4-5, CEB

"Researchers aggregated 59 years of research, encompassing more than 19,000 participants and 136 studies from lab, business, and classroom settings. They discovered that while the gender gap has narrowed in recent decades, it still persists . . . We found showing sensitivity and concern for others—stereotypically feminine traits—made someone less likely to be seen as a leader. However, it's those same characteristics that make leaders effective. Thus, because of this unconscious bias against communal traits, organizations may unintentionally select the wrong people for leadership roles, choosing individuals who are loud and confident but lack the ability to support their followers' development and success. The researchers suggest promoting the value of communal behaviors in performance evaluations, prompting quieter individuals to share their ideas, and being mindful of any unconscious biases a manager or staff may have." (Matthew Biddle, "Many Don't See Women as Leaders at Work")

PRAYER

Creator of all that is good and blessed, guide me so that I may see the true person of worth. Help me to embrace all of your creation as equal and right.

How do you ensure that you have no blind spots
and see all the people in your care?

— 5 —
FOLLOWING THOSE WE TRUST

"Trust the LORD and do good; live in the land,
and farm faithfulness."

Psalm 37:3, CEB

We all follow someone, and we only willingly follow persons we trust. But trust can only happen when there is a solid relationship between leaders and followers. Following any leader is costly because it means change, which can create risk, uncertainty, and vulnerability, whether the path leads to a new worship schedule, corporate restructuring, a decision to hire an unorthodox professor at a college, or an incursion into unknown territory. Trust allows followers to accept proposed actions more readily because trust in leaders they know has the effect of reducing the anxiety associated with perceived risk and uncertainty in the proposed course of action. (Adapted from Herminia Ibarra, Robin Ely, and Deborah Kolb, "Women Rising: The Unseen Barriers")

PRAYER

God, I go, and I do, because my total trust is in you. You have never disappointed me. Help me to know my people and for them to know me so we may trust one another enough to go forward in confidence.

Who do you trust to follow?

How trustworthy are you?

— 6 —
TRUE LEADERS FAIL

"My body and my heart fail, but God is
my heart's rock and my share forever."

Psalm 73:26, CEB

"We will have our share of darkness and will fail at times. As a matter of fact, the more we care and the greater the scope of our compassion, the more this will occur. It is a basic statistical probability. The more we are involved, the more we raise the odds that we will fail. It is as simple as that. Consequently, our perspective on failure is essential. This is not only important for us who are in 'official' caregiving and mentoring roles but also for those who count on us to remain involved—especially when the odds are great against us succeeding as we would naturally like to do. Our *attitude* is key in failure and a sense of loss when our goals are not achieved." (Robert J. Wicks, *Night Call: Embracing Compassion and Hope in a Troubled World*)

PRAYER

God, only you do not fail. Help me to accept my failures as part of trying and learning. Help me to grow from them and not harm others.

What have you learned from your failures?

—7—
DISCOVER STRENGTH IN KINDNESS

"May the LORD reward your efforts! May your acts
of kindness be repaid fully by the LORD God of
Israel, from whom you have sought protection."

Ruth 2:12, NET

"The lesson was clear: Don't just show kindness in passion or to be courteous. Show it in depth, show it with passion, and expect nothing in return. Kindness is not just about being nice; it's about recognizing another human being who deserves care and respect. . . . It ain't brain surgery. Every person in an organization has value and wants that value to be recognized. Every human being needs appreciation and reinforcement. The person who came to clean my office each night was no less a person than the President, a general, or a cabinet member. They deserved and got from me a thank-you, a kind word, an inquiry that let him or her know their value. I wanted them to know they weren't just janitors. I couldn't do my job without them, and the department relied on them. There are no trivial jobs in any successful organization. But there are all too many trivial leaders who don't understand this oh so simple and easy-to-apply principle." (Colin Powell, *It Worked for Me: In Life and Leadership*)

PRAYER

Gracious God, you have been so kind to me despite my failures and disappointments. You have given me so many blessings I did not deserve. Help my kindness be reflected to those I lead and engage every day.

Who needs your kindness today?

——1——
THE DANGER OF CARING

"Cast your burden on the LORD—he will support you!
God will never let the righteous be shaken!"

Psalm 55:22, CEB

"The seeds of burnout and the seeds of enthusiasm are in reality the same seeds. The commitment to others and to our work that fuels our enthusiasm can be the same energy that causes us to ignore our own needs and inadvertently depletes our inner resources. And so, anyone who truly cares can expect that they will need to ride the waves of burnout—and occasionally get knocked down by a wave they missed! . . . Central to such action is a willingness to reorient priorities and take risks with our style of dealing with the world, which for some reason is not working optimally. To accomplish this, frequently our mentor and colleagues need to become involved." (Robert J. Wicks, *Bounce: Living the Resilient Life*)

PRAYER

Sustainer of my mind, body, and soul, hear this prayer. Help me to keep the fire of passion, care, and faith alive within me. Nudge me when I should slow down and rest from my labors so I may serve you fully.

Who on your team is burned out?

What can you do to avoid losing your passion for ministry?

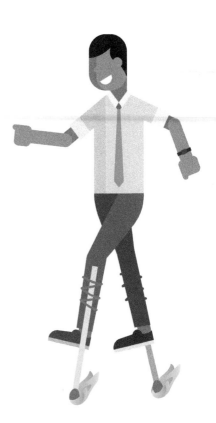

— 2 —
DISCOVER YOUR SELF-AWARENESS

"Be careful that you don't practice your religion in front of people to draw their attention. If you do, you will have no reward from your Father who is in heaven."

Matthew 6:1, CEB

"Unsurprisingly, self-awareness is omnipresent in leadership models. After all, leaders are tasked with influencing and engaging their teams, so it is essential that they understand how their behaviors impact other people. For example, leaders need to decide whether positive or negative feedback is more effective in motivating an underperforming employee; how best to communicate their vision in order to provide followers with a meaningful mission and sense of purpose; and how to act as brand ambassadors for their organizations. None of these things can be accomplished effectively unless leaders are able to predict how their actions will be perceived by their followers, teams, and organizations. . . . Be the lens through which your boss can have a better understanding of the workplace. However, it is key that you suggest this with tact rather than bluntly imposing your views on your boss." (Tomas Chamorro-Premuzic, "How to Work for a Boss Who Lacks Self-Awareness")

PRAYER

God of my life, reveal yourself to me so I may see myself through your eyes. I seek truth so I may share truth with those whom I lead. Help me to lead with honesty and integrity.

Who can give you honest feedback about
how you come across to others?

— 3 —
BEING FUTURE-FOCUSED

"I'm sure about this: the one who started a
good work in you will stay with you to complete
the job by the day of Christ Jesus."

Philippians 1:6, CEB

"Being future-focused is crucial for a leader and that applies to careers as well as companies. It means immersing ourselves in learning experiences that probably won't feel comfortable and being opportunistic and nimble with that new knowledge. How many gifted leaders are about to put a ceiling on their own potential because they're having trouble seeing around the corner?" (John Ryan, President and CEO, Center for Creative Leadership)

PRAYER

God, I can envision and make a best guess of what the future holds, but you alone know its secrets. As I walk down this unsure path not knowing the dangers, watch over me. Open my faith and my understanding.

Do you tend to be more hopeful or fearful?
How does this affect your team?

—4—
MAKING HARD DECISIONS WITH GOOD JUDGMENT

"And this I pray, that your love may abound
still more and more in real knowledge and all
discernment, so that you may approve the things
that are excellent, in order to be sincere and
blameless until the day of Christ."

Philippians 1:9-10, NASB

"Gray areas are particularly risky today because of the seductive power of analytical technique. Many of the hard problems now facing managers and companies require sophisticated techniques for analyzing vast amounts of information. It is tempting to think that if you can just get the right information and use the right analytics, you can make the right decision. It can also be tempting to hide out from tough decisions or disguise the exercise of power by telling other people that the numbers tell the whole story and there is no choice about what to think or do. But serious problems are usually gray. By themselves, tools and techniques won't give you answers. You have to use your judgment and make hard choices." (Joseph Badaracco, "Timeless Advice for Making a Hard Choice")

PRAYER

God, there are so many choices to consider and the impact many times is so serious. It sometimes creates a fear of failure that consumes me. I lean on you for your counsel and wisdom. Strengthen me with confidence to move forward.

What hard decisions are on your horizon?

What help might you require?

25

5

EXPECTATIONS FOR
TRANSFORMATION

"The Spirit of the LORD will come powerfully
upon you, and you will prophesy with them; and you
will be changed into a different person."

1 Samuel 10:6, NIV

"Few leaders would disagree that personal transformation is an important building block of any successful change effort. Unfortunately, too many leaders want transformation to happen at unrealistic speeds, with minimal effort, and everywhere but within themselves. As Manfred Kets de Vries says in *The Leader on the Couch*, 'Organizations the world over are full of people who are unable to recognize repetitive behavior patterns that have become dysfunctional.' This reflects an endemic lack of self-awareness in leadership, and the costs are significant. One study found that when it comes to decision making, coordination, and conflict management, teams that have a low degree of self-awareness are less than half as effective as teams that are highly self-aware." (Ron Carucci, "Organizations Can't Change If Leaders Can't Change with Them")

PRAYER

You, O God, know me more than I know myself; examine me to see where I need to change, and transform me into a person that better reflects your image. Help me recognize I am still in the process of being created by you.

How have you changed or not changed
over the last five years?

27

— 6 —
POWERED UP TO GO THE EXTRA MILE

"I've commanded you to be brave and strong, haven't I? Don't be alarmed or terrified, because the LORD your God is with you wherever you go."

Joshua 1:9, CEB

"Empowered people give it their all, even on their worst days. They're always pushing themselves to go the extra mile. One of Bruce Lee's pupils ran three miles every day with him. One day, they were about to hit the three-mile mark when Bruce said, 'Let's do two more.' His pupil was tired and said, 'I'll die if I run two more.' Bruce's response? 'Then do it.' His pupil became so angry that he finished the full five miles. Exhausted and furious, he confronted Bruce about his comment, and Bruce explained it this way: 'Quit and you might as well be dead. If you always put limits on what you can do, physical or anything else, it'll spread over into the rest of your life. It'll spread into your work, into your morality, into your entire being. There are no limits. There are plateaus, but you must not stay there; you must go beyond them. If it kills you, it kills you. A man must constantly exceed his level.' If you aren't getting a little bit better each day, then you're most likely getting a little worse—and what kind of life is that?" (Travis Bradberry, "Here's Why Your Attitude Is More Important Than Your Intelligence")

PRAYER

Dear God, I sometimes grow weary and uncertain. Doubt and fear creep silently into my heart and soul. Empower me with courage and resiliency to persevere.

Where do you need God right now?

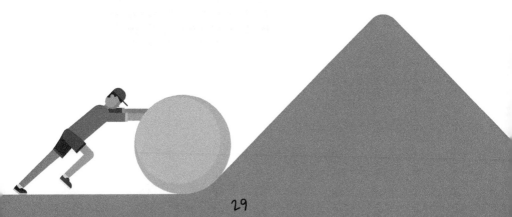

—7—
DISCOVER PEOPLE: CALL THEM BY NAME

"You must not deal unjustly in judgment: you must neither show partiality to the poor nor honor the rich. You must judge your fellow citizen fairly."

Leviticus 19:15, NET

"Studies have shown that you can improve service by 80 percent if you address people by their first name. Why would anyone want to miss that opportunity, in work or in life? To not do that is the opposite of shrewd, not to mention the opposite of how we should be treating our fellow human beings. As a leader, addressing people in the workplace, personalizing our communication with them in the hallways, even down in the parking garage, that's just the tip of the iceberg when it comes to caring for your people." (Rick Lynch, *Adapt or Die: Leadership Principles from an American General*)

PRAYER

God, you call me by name. You see me as your child. I bow in humility and gratitude. Give me the spirit of care to see all people as your children, each important in your sight.

30

Who are you tempted to favor? to ignore?
to placate? to avoid? How is this
hurting your leadership?

HELLO
my name is

RAY

LLO
name is

Kyle

HELLO
my name is

Linda

31

—1—
DISCOVER FAMILY AS PART OF YOUR EQUATION

"A house torn apart by divisions will collapse."

Mark 3:25, CEB

"Wanting a serious career was a huge incentive for me to change, but the idea of family was the primary motivator. Far too often people use their family commitments as an excuse to stay where they are, but family should be a tool that drives you to do better and push harder. . . . That kind of leadership applies across the board. We might be a family or a community or a business, but we are also a group of individuals, and leaders are role models for that group. That's how I treat everyone. I want people to follow me by what I do, not what I tell them to do." (John Addison, "Leadership Lessons I Learned from My Family")

PRAYER

God, I am so glad I am part of your family. I belong to you. Help me to see my family as a blessing and not lose sight of their central place in my life.

How is your family doing? What do they need from you?

—2—
DISCOVER STEPS TO LEADERSHIP

"You are the one who created my innermost
parts; you knit me together while I
was still in my mother's womb."

Psalm 139:13, CEB

1. Reflection leads to resolution. 2. Resolution leads to perspective. 3. Perspective leads to point of view. 4. Point of view leads to tests and measures. 5. Tests and measures lead to desire. 6. Desire leads to mastery. 7. Mastery leads to strategic thinking. 8. Strategic thinking leads to full self-expression. 9. The synthesis of full self-expression = leadership. (Adapted from Warren Bennis, *On Becoming a Leader*)

PRAYER

God of all creation, mold and shape my thoughts that I may be more benevolent to those in crisis, more forgiving for those who forgive me, and more gracious to others who do not accept me. These things I ask in order to lead those you have given me.

Where are you on the path to leadership?

3

ROADBLOCKS AND OBSTACLES == OPPORTUNITY

"So then, let's work for the good of all whenever
we have an opportunity, and especially for
those in the household of faith."

Galatians 6:10, CEB

Journalist Sally Deneen tells this story: "Long before 5-foot-2 Frances Hesselbein became sought out by Army generals and White House chiefs-of-staff for her leadership advice, she was a young married mom in Johnstown, Pennsylvania, fending off requests that she lead a 30-member Girl Scout troop that otherwise would disband. 'In my life, I don't have roadblocks and obstacles,' Hesselbein said. 'I might have something you would call a challenge. I throw that out the window, and I call that a wonderful opportunity. When you see a roadblock or challenge as an opportunity, it is amazing how you are already halfway there,' says Hesselbein. 'It helps to have your blood type B positive,' she quipped. 'That's my private joke, and it's true.'" (Sally Deneen, "Women Who Leaned In")

PRAYER

God of all the possible, remind me daily that all challenges I face through faith and attitude become an opportunity to rise to a higher level of success and an opportunity to do good.

How do you exercise your leadership
so that it is good for all?

— 4 —
REASONS FOR
POOR DECISIONS

"If any of you lacks wisdom, let him
ask God, who gives generously to all without
reproach, and it will be given him."

James 1:5, ESV

In their classic article Jack Zenger and Joseph Folkman cite nine factors that lead to poor decision making. Here they are from most to least significant: laziness; not anticipating the unexpected; indecisiveness; staying locked in the past; having no strategic alignment; overdependence; isolation; lack of technical depth; and failure to communicate the what, where, and when. (Adapted from Jack Zenger and Joseph Folkman, "Nine Habits That Lead to Terrible Decisions")

PRAYER

God of perfection and wisdom, bring wisdom to my decisions as I lead your people placed in my care. Keep my spirit humble.

What wisdom could you share with those you lead?

—5—
EXPECT THE UNEXPECTED

"Take heed to yourselves, lest your hearts become burdened by excessiveness and drunkenness and anxieties of life, and that day comes on you unexpectedly."

Luke 21:34, MEV

"We develop our plans by answering six questions for each set goal:

1. What needs to be accomplished?
2. Why does it need to be done? (How does it contribute to our overall mission?)
3. When does it need to be accomplished?
4. Where am I/are we now in relation to the goal?
5. Who will be involved in accomplishing this?
6. How will it be accomplished? (What specific steps and activities are involved, and what resources are required?)

After answering these questions with as much detail as possible, we perform the last of the planning activities: adding contingencies. We do our best to anticipate the unexpected by asking 'But what if' questions. . . . Certainly we can't predict all the obstacles we may face, but combining some thought with past experiences does enhance our readiness to deal with that fellow Murphy's Law." (Eric Harvey, *The Leadership Lessons of Santa Claus: How to Get Big Things Done in Your Workshop*)

PRAYER

God, we know what to expect from you: goodness, mercy, forgiveness, and strength for the journey. Help me to be always ready for the unexpected things so I may do what is good in your sight.

What has surprised you recently or caught you off guard?

6

CREATING A STRONG ORGANIZATIONAL CULTURE

"Look at the birds of the air: they neither sow nor reap nor gather into barns, and yet your heavenly Father feeds them. Are you not of more value than they?"

Matthew 6:26, ESV

"When looking to change the culture dramatically and develop values that are in line with customers, clients, and supply chain partners, organizations need to start with their leadership—not only present leadership, but future leadership as well. One senior executive shares his views: 'Managing across diverse businesses, cultures, and geographies is a major challenge. There are tensions between different geographies in a global firm—some are natural because of different backgrounds and perspectives; others are exacerbated by external political tensions. I believe finding common ground around the organization's mission and values is the key. . . . We need to embrace diversity without divisiveness and stay focused on a shared vision of success, which is how we create value and deliver results to our clients and people, and on a common set of values, which is what we stand for and how we behave as an institution. I believe this is the mark of an enduring institution—they create value and are based on values.'" (Donna Brooks and Lynn Brooks, *Ten Secrets of Successful Leaders: The Strategies, Skills, and Knowledge Leaders at Every Level Need to Succeed*)

PRAYER

God, create within me acceptance, respect, and the ability to see the value of people over business. Shape my thinking so that my leadership position will be balanced and healthy.

42

What are the three primary values that undergird your leadership?

7

DISCOVER WHERE YOU ARE INDISPENSABLE

"This is the list of the descendants of Adam.
When God created humankind, he made them in
the likeness of God. Male and female he created
them, and he blessed them and named them
'Humankind' when they were created."

Genesis 5:1-2, NRSV

"No one is indispensable or irreplaceable at work . . . anyone from the lowliest yard worker to the highest executive could easily be replaced and few tears would be shed. The most important position in the U.S.—the Presidency—is rotated every four years with little mourning. But try replacing a son or daughter, a mother or father, a husband or wife without grave psychological damage. For it's in our homes that we are needed; it's in our family that we are important." (Peter Blitchington and Robert Cruise, *Understanding Your Temperament: A Self-Analysis with a Christian Viewpoint*)

PRAYER

God, I get so caught up in life outside my home that it steals my energy, empathy, and love. I give my leftovers. Help me to reflect that kind of love to those you have given me in care.

Who is indispensable to you? to your ministry?

45

—1—
THE PATH TO SUCCESS IS FAILURE

"Do not lie in wait like an outlaw against the home of the
righteous; do no violence to the place where the righteous
live; for though they fall seven times, they will rise again;
but the wicked are overthrown by calamity."

Proverbs 24:15-16, NRSV

"The signature of the truly great versus the merely successful is not the absence of
difficulty, but the ability to come back from setbacks, even cataclysmic catastrophes,
stronger than before. . . . The path out of darkness begins with those exasperatingly
persistent individuals who are constitutionally incapable of capitulation. It's one
thing to suffer a staggering defeat . . . and entirely another to give up on the values
and aspirations that make the protracted struggle worthwhile. Failure is not so much
a physical state as a state of mind; success is falling down, and getting up one more
time, without end." (Jim Collins, *How the Mighty Fall: And Why Some Companies
Never Give In*)

PRAYER

God of my soul, sometimes all I see is failure and setbacks. Give me strength to
stay the course and have faith in myself and in you. Encourage my spirit to get
back up again.

What is one failure that eventually resulted in a success?

What did you learn?

— 2 —
VISION CHANGES THE WORLD

"Where there is no vision, the people perish:
but he that keepeth the law, happy is he."

Proverbs 29:18, KJV

"Some believe there is nothing one man or woman can do against the enormous array of the world's ills—against misery, against ignorance, or injustice and violence. Yet many of the world's great movements, of thought and action, have flowed from the work of a single man. A young monk began the Protestant reformation, a young general extended an empire from Macedonia to the borders of the earth, and a young woman reclaimed the territory of France. It was a young Italian explorer who discovered the New World, and the thirty-year-old Thomas Jefferson who proclaimed that all men are created equal. 'Give me a place to stand,' said Archimedes, 'and I will move the world.' These men moved the world, and so can we all." (The Poynter Institute, *The Kennedys: America's Front-Page Family*)

PRAYER

"Disturb us, Lord, when we are too well pleased with ourselves, when our dreams have come true because we have dreamed too little, when we arrive safely because we have sailed too close to the shore." —Sir Frances Drake

What vision do you have for your ministry?
Short-term? Long-term?

—3—
FIND TIME FOR SOLITUDE AND THINKING

"God, the one and only—I'll wait as long as he says.
Everything I need comes from him, so why not?
He's solid rock under my feet, breathing room for my
soul, an impregnable castle: I'm set for life."

Psalm 62:1-2, The Message

The volume of information and stimuli coming at us every day makes it more difficult than ever to focus. To do the careful thinking that decision making and leadership require, you must step back from the noise of the world. Schedule fifteen-minute breaks at least once or twice a day to sit quietly in your office or take a walk. Commit to these breaks as you would any meeting or appointment; if you don't schedule moments of quiet, something else will fill the time. Use them to think about your to-do list, especially the tasks you should stop doing. Solitude gives you the space to reflect on where your time is best spent. Try to get clarity on which meetings you should stop attending, which committees you should step down from, and which invitations you should politely decline. (Adapted from Mike Erwin, "In a Distracted World, Solitude Is a Competitive Advantage")

PRAYER

God of my alone time, allow me to still my mind and heart so I may hear and see you. As I lead in noise and actions, may my heart be quietly in union with you.

Where and when do you do your best thinking?
How much time do you spend alone with God?

—4—
WHEN YOU AREN'T FEELING CONFIDENT

"You will not be afraid when you go to bed, and you will sleep soundly through the night. You will not have to worry about sudden disasters, such as come on the wicked like a storm. The LORD will keep you safe. He will not let you fall into a trap."

Proverbs 3:24-26, GNT

"You can project confidence by doing four things. First, demonstrate empathy for your team members. They want to know that you aren't out of touch with what they're feeling. Second, communicate your vision for the team—and that's a tough challenge. People need to have a clear sense of where they are headed. Third, set a direction for the team. Show them how you'll reach the vision together. Last, give people proof. They need a reason to buy in to what you're telling them, so offer evidence for your direction and optimism. Be specific, be personal, and reference the work that the team is already doing. This will build your team's confidence—and your own." (Peter Bregman, "How to Lead When You're Feeling Afraid")

PRAYER

God, you are my rock in whom I find my strength and confidence to go forward. Although I may have doubts and fears, I know you will never leave me and will sustain me.

52

What keeps you up at night?

—5—

A LEADER'S WORD

"I will not agree that you are right. Until my dying day, I won't give up my integrity."

Job 27:5, CEB

"Though frustrated by Lincoln's slowness in issuing the [Emancipation Proclamation], the abolitionist leader Frederick Douglass had come to believe that Lincoln was not a man 'to reconsider, retract, and contradict words and purposes solemnly proclaimed.' Correctly, he judged that Lincoln would 'take no step backward,' that 'if he has taught us to confide in nothing else, he has taught us to confide in his word.'" (Doris Kearns Goodwin, "Lincoln and the Art of Transformative Leadership")

PRAYER

God, whose word never wavers, I will never doubt you. Help me so others who depend on me will know my word and my integrity stand strong and will not falter.

Recall a time when you could not keep your word.
What were the repercussions?

— 6 —
THE POWER OF EGO

*"Pride goes before destruction,
and a haughty spirit before a fall."*

Proverbs 16:18, ESV

Here are some tips to help you break free of an inflated ego.

• Consider the perks and privileges you are being offered in your role. Some of them enable you to do your job effectively. But some of them are simply perks to promote your status and power and ultimately your ego. Consider which of your privileges you can let go of.

• Support, develop, and work with people who won't feed your ego. Hire smart people with the confidence to speak up.

• Humility and gratitude are the cornerstone of selflessness. Make a habit of taking a moment each day to reflect on the people that were part of making you successful.

(Adapted from Rasmus Hougaard and Jacqueline Carter, "Ego Is the Enemy of Good Leadership")

PRAYER

God, without you, I am nothing. All that I have and have done is because of you. Help me to be selfless and portray humility to those I lead.

Who keeps you humble? Why?

—7—
LEADING THE PEOPLE PROCESS

"Save your people and bless your inheritance;

be their shepherd and carry them forever."

Psalm 28:9, NIV

"The people process is more important than either the strategy or operations processes. After all, it's the people of an organization who make judgments about how markets are changing, create strategies based on those judgments, and translate the strategies into operational realities. To put it simply and starkly: If you don't get the people process right, you will never fulfill the potential of your business." (Larry Bossidy and Ram Charan, *Execution: The Discipline of Getting Things Done*)

PRAYER

God and Savior, you are the master of loving care; you care for me every step I take, lifting me up when I stumble. Open my heart to those whom I lead that I treat them as people of value.

What are the characteristics of
a good shepherd? How do you stack up?

CLAIM

—1—
CLAIM YOUR LEADERSHIP

"Warriors were scarce, they were scarce in Israel,
until you arose, Deborah, until you arose as
a motherly protector in Israel."

Judges 5:7, NET

"I didn't love being the only woman in the room, but I was also okay with it. And I learned to not think about how I was different. I think in many situations growing up, I was the only immigrant, or I was the only Chinese-American in a room or in my school. And I learned to either not notice or to embrace it as a positive and to use it to bring something new, and different, and fresh to the group. And I think that comfort with being different is so important for anyone who wants to disrupt because the whole idea is to not conform to what everyone else is already doing." (Clara Shih, "10 Powerful Quotes from Female Leaders on International Women's Day")

PRAYER

Wise Counselor, help me to see myself as good and worthy of your confidence. Guard me that I not conform to other's expectations but only seek to please you.

Who do you feel obligated to protect? Who protects you?

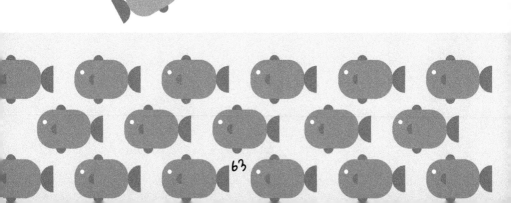

— 2 —
RESET AFTER FAILURE

"For judgment, resulting from the one transgression, led to condemnation, but the gracious gift from the many failures led to justification."

Romans 5:16, NET

Alison Beard: "Yea, there've definitely been some huge setbacks that you've had in your life, not least, the presidential election. So once something like that happens, how do you reset?"

John Kerry: "Well, I think you look at what the alternative is, and you have to consciously decide that's a stupid alternative. . . . I was not going to stop . . . the issues we wanted to advance, the agenda that we were pursuing . . . people who are going to fight for it, people are going to continue. So, the idea of just crying in my teacup and disappearing and becoming a hermit or pulling away from the field seemed to me to be a pretty stupid choice. And I just consciously decided I'm not going there. I'm going back to work." ("John Kerry on Leadership, Compromise, and Change")

PRAYER

God who does not fail, help me in my failures. Lift me up from the dust and strengthen me to continue the journey.

Think of a time you were knocked down.
How did you reset and get back up?

3

CLAIMING OUR EMOTIONAL INFLUENCE

"Guard your heart above all else, for it
determines the course of your life."

Proverbs 4:23, NLT

"Great leaders move us. They ignite our passion and inspire the best in us. When we try to explain why they are so effective, we speak of strategy, vision, or powerful ideas. But the reality is much more primal: great leadership works through the emotions. . . . Leaders typically talked more than anyone else, and what they said was listened to more carefully. . . . But the impact on emotions goes beyond what a leader says. In these studies, even when leaders were not talking, they were watched more carefully than anyone else in the group. When people raised a question for the group as a whole, they would keep their eyes on the leader to see his or her emotional reaction as the most valid response, and so model their own on it—particularly in an ambiguous situation, where various members react differently. In a sense, the leader sets the emotional standard." (Daniel Goleman, Richard Boyatzis, and Annie McKee, *Primal Leadership: Unleashing the Power of Emotional Intelligence*)

PRAYER

Dear God, I cast my eyes upon you to receive strength and courage. Please watch over me and guard my heart so that those I lead may feel encouragement and affirmation.

66

Who inspires you?
What are you passionate about?

67

—4—
BEING ACCOUNTABLE
TO EACH OTHER

"And let us consider how to provoke one another to love and good deeds, not neglecting to meet together, as is the habit of some, but encouraging one another, and all the more as you see the Day approaching."

Hebrews 10:24-25, NRSV

"*Accountability* is a buzzword that has lost much of its meaning as it has become as overused as terms like *empowerment* and *quality*. In the context of teamwork, however, it refers specifically to the willingness of team members to call their peers on performance or behaviors that might hurt the team. The essence of this dysfunction is the unwillingness of team members to tolerate the interpersonal discomfort that accompanies calling a peer on his or her behavior and the more general tendency to avoid difficult conversations. Members of great teams overcome these natural inclinations, opting to 'enter the danger' with one another." (Patrick Lencioni, *The Five Dysfunctions of a Team: A Leadership Fable*)

PRAYER

God, you hold me accountable for my deeds. You see all. Nothing is hidden. Help me to be accountable to myself and as a leader for others.

How do you feel about those to whom you are accountable?
How do you treat those who are accountable to you?

5

LEADERS WITH HEART

"Because our message of the gospel came to you not in word only, but also in power and in the Holy Spirit and with full conviction, just as you know what kind of persons we proved to be among you for your sake."

1 Thessalonians 1:5, NRSV

"To understand why convictions and courage are essential to success, you must recognize that many beat-up people walk through your office doors every day. . . . Heart is the difference maker in great leaders. You cannot be a great coach without heart. If you don't genuinely care about people—if you are coldly tactical and distantly technical and efficiently process-oriented and you leave your heart out of it—then your people will follow you only part of the way. They need to believe that by following you, they will go places they would not even see without you at the helm. Heart is the home to both convictions and courage; it is the fuel of all exceptional leaders. Your beliefs about your people and their potential inevitably impact your success or failure as a leader." (Daniel Harkavy, *Becoming a Coaching Leader: A Proven System of Building Your Team of Champions*)

PRAYER

God, whose love and passion for me is unfathomable, stir within me a heart filled with courage and conviction to do the right thing no matter the consequence. Let me not waver in compassion for those you have placed in my care.

Reflect on one of your convictions.
How does it affect your leadership?

— 6 —
STRIVING TO PERFECTION

"All have sinned and fall short of God's glory."

Romans 3:23, CEB

"Vince Lombardi, the late, great Green Bay Packers football coach, used to tell his teams, 'Gentlemen, we are going to relentlessly chase perfection, knowing full well we will not catch it, because nothing is perfect. But we are going to relentlessly chase it, because in the process we will catch excellence.' We will never arrive as the perfect servant leader. (If you think you have arrived, you now have some humility issues you need to look at!) The goal of any aspiring leader (whether manager, parent, spouse, coach or teacher) should not be perfection, rather continuous improvement—being able to say every few months, 'I'm not where I want to be, but I am better than I used to be.'" (James C. Hunter, *The Servant: A Simple Story about the True Essence of Leadership*)

PRAYER

God, you are perfect. Help me strive to be the best leader and person I can. I know I make mistakes and fail, but be by my side as my strength and redeem my shortcomings.

Take a few minutes and reflect on the state of your soul.

—7—
EARNED TRUST

"Trust in the LORD with all your heart and lean not on your own understanding; in all your ways submit to him, and he will make your paths straight."

Proverbs 3:5-6, NIV

"Trust does not emerge simply because a seller makes a rational case why the customer should buy a product or service, or because an executive promises change. Trust is not a checklist. Fulfilling all your responsibilities does not create trust. Trust is a feeling, not a rational experience. We trust some people and companies even when things go wrong, and we don't trust others even though everything might have gone exactly as it should have. A completed checklist does not guarantee trust. Trust begins to emerge when we have a sense that another person or organization is driven by things other than their own self-gain." (Simon Sinek, *Start with Why: How Great Leaders Inspire Everyone to Take Action*)

PRAYER

God who has my full trust, I quietly listen for your direction and affirmation. Humble me to receive the trust of those whom I lead. Remind me that trust is earned.

What is an area where you need to increase your understanding? How can you address it?

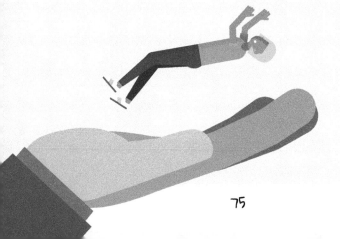

— 1 —
LEADING DESPITE CRITICISM

"Whoever heeds life-giving correction
will be at home among the wise."

Proverbs 15:31, NIV

"You need to cultivate a thick skin to deal with unwarranted criticism. You also need to go about your business without responding to your critics. Trying to explain the reasons for your actions will not satisfy your critics, but it will distract you from your work. Success is the way to silence criticism." (Al Kaltman, *Cigars, Whiskey, and Winning: Leadership Lessons from General Ulysses S. Grant*)

PRAYER

Loving God, strengthen my resolve in believing in myself and decisions despite the voices of doubt. But humble me to hear wise counsel.

Reflect on a time when you graciously received criticism.
Reflect on a time when criticism was
especially hard to take and why.

2

A TRUSTWORTHY LEADER

"The LORD rewarded me for my godly deeds; he took notice of my blameless behavior. You prove to be loyal to one who is faithful; you prove to be trustworthy to one who is innocent."

Psalm 18:24-25, NET

"Being or becoming trustworthy cannot be reduced to pure behaviors. You can't bottle it in a competency model. Our actions are driven by our beliefs, and our beliefs are driven by our values or principles. Trustworthy behavior is way too complex to fake without the beliefs and values behind them. If your values don't drive you to behave in a trustworthy manner all the time, you'll be found out quickly." (Trusted Advisor, LLC, "Trust in Business: The Core Concepts")

PRAYER

God, you are above any doubt. Your trustworthiness is above reproach. I can depend on you. Help me to be trusted by you and by those in my charge.

Do you practice what you preach in terms of your leadership? Why or why not?

3

PRINCIPLES OF
TRUSTWORTHY BEHAVIOR

"The Lord detests lying lips, but he delights
in those who tell the truth."

Proverbs 12:22, NLT

1. A *focus on the Other* (client, customer, internal coworker, boss, partner, subordinate) for the Other's sake, not just as a means to one's own ends.

2. A *collaborative* approach to relationships. Collaboration here means a willingness to work together, creating joint goals and joint approaches to getting there.

3. A *medium- to long-term* relationship perspective, not a short-term transactional focus. The most profitable relationships for both parties are those where multiple transactions over time are assumed in the approach to each transaction.

4. A habit of being *transparent* in all one's dealings.

(Adapted from Trusted Advisor, LLC, "Trust in Business: The Core Concepts")

PRAYER

Holy God, as my leader, you have called me to be your trusting servant. Help me be a positive force to inspire and build trust and confidence in all persons for your glory.

Why is it hard for some people to tell the truth?

Why might it be hard for some people
to tell you the truth?

81

—4—
POWER VS. RESPECT

"For this reason I am writing this while I am away from you: When I come I do not want to be severe in using the authority the Lord gave me to build you up and not to tear you down."

2 Corinthians 13:10, ISV

"Leaders have legal authority over followers. They can demand and expect obedience on the job and have the power to take action against followers who do not obey or meet expected standards of performance. They can fire them. They can dock their pay. They can demote them. In the military, we have severe punishment for disobeying orders. Obedience alone may get the job done, but probably doesn't inspire commitment to the job. It doesn't necessarily inspire pride in the work or the product or a passion for excellence. These come when followers feel they are part of a well-led team. And this comes when they respect their leaders and when they, in turn, believe that they are respected by their leaders. It comes when they trust their leaders, and when they believe they are trusted by their leaders. They have to know they have value." (Colin Powell, *It Worked for Me: In Life and Leadership*)

PRAYER

Dear God, we know all power and authority comes from you. Let me use what you have given to me wisely.

What does it mean to have authority over another person?
How do you feel about those who have authority over you?

— 5 —
INTERESTED ENOUGH
TO LISTEN

*"Cease straying, my child, from the words of knowledge,
in order that you may hear instruction."*

Proverbs 19:27, NRSV

"Leaders must be interested in others—and what they have to say. They have to be curious and empathetic. As a leader—and we're talking leadership at all levels, from leading your first team to the CEO—one needs to be a dynamic, active listener, asking questions, gathering information, talking to customers to see what they have to say, and talking to employees to hear their issues. It's what most talented employees expect—and they will subtly remind leaders of this point—if they don't like your organizational culture, they'll go somewhere else. Good leaders know that buy-in and collaboration are essential to making things happen, and listening to the needs and perspectives of customers, employees, and others is key. You need to get at the pulse point of what they want." (Donna Brooks and Lynn Brooks, *Ten Secrets of Successful Leaders: The Strategies, Skills, and Knowledge Leaders at Every Level Need to Succeed*)

PRAYER

Listener who hears all my words, both spoken and unspoken, help me to quiet down to hear the needs of others. Open my ears to truly respond with caring.

What can you do to improve your listening skills?

—6—
THE RIGHT POWER

"I can do all things through Christ
which strengtheneth me."

Philippians 4:13, KJV

"In order to motivate others, managers must be motivated themselves. The key issue here is the *source* of the motivation—the way the manager defines success. Some equate success with personal achievement; some see it as being liked by others. In order to succeed in a complex organization, a manager needs to have a *power motivation*, which is not a dictatorial impulse but rather the desire to have impact, to be strong and influential. This power must be disciplined and channeled in ways that benefit the organization, not the manager himself [herself]." (David C. McClelland and David H. Burnham, "Power Is the Great Motivator")

PRAYER

God who has all power, guard my heart and mind that the power given to me by my position be one of balance and humility. Let me use my power for selfless ends.

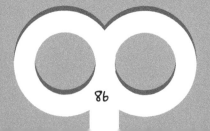

What motivates you?

What kills your motivation?

What works for you to motivate other people?

7
WHAT GREAT LEADERS DO

"The Lord replied, 'Who then is the faithful and wise manager, whom the master puts in charge of his household servants, to give them their allowance of food at the proper time?'"

Luke 12:42, NET

"Great leaders discover what is universal and capitalize on it. Their job is to rally people toward a better future. Leaders can succeed in this only when they can cut through differences of race, sex, age, nationality, and personality and, using stories and celebrating heroes, tap into those very few needs we all share. The job of a manager, meanwhile, is to turn one person's particular talent into performance. Managers will succeed only when they can identify and deploy the differences among people, challenging each employee to excel in his or her own way. This doesn't mean a leader can't be a manager or vice versa. But to excel at one or both, you must be aware of the very different skills each role requires." (Marcus Buckingham, "What Great Managers Do")

PRAYER

God who knows me in all ways, open my heart and mind to truly see people for who they are in all their uniqueness and possibilities. You have given them to me to lead and nurture. Help me succeed.

What differences have you had to cut through in your context? How did it go?

—1—
LEADING WITH
RIGHTEOUSNESS AND HONOR

"He has told you, O mortal, what is good; and what does
the LORD require of you but to do justice, and to love
kindness, and to walk humbly with your God?"

Micah 6:8, NRSV

"There can be no nobler cause for which to work than the peace of righteousness; and
high honor is due those serene and lofty souls who with wisdom and courage, with
high idealism tempered by sane facing of the actual facts of life, have striven to bring
nearer the day when armed strife between nation and nation, between man and man
shall end throughout the world. The men [and women] who have stood highest in our
history, as in the history of all countries, are those who scorned injustice, who were
incapable of oppressing the weak, or of permitting their country, with their consent,
to oppress the weak, but who did not hesitate to draw the sword when to leave it
undrawn meant inability to arrest triumphant wrong." (Theodore Roosevelt, *Theodore
Roosevelt: An Autobiography*)

PRAYER

God, build a wall of strength around my convictions and beliefs that they remain
steadfast. Let me do justice, love kindness, and walk humbly with you.

How can you improve your ministry processes and procedures to make them more just and equitable?

—2—
CREATIVITY IN CHAOS

"For God is not the author of confusion,
but of peace, as in all churches of the saints."

1 Corinthians 14:33, MEV

"A few years ago, the psychologist Daniel Oppenheimer asked some high school teachers to reformat the handouts they were giving to some of their classes. The regular handout would be formatted in something straightforward, such as Helvetica. But half these classes were getting handouts that were formatted in something sort of intense, like Haettenschweiler, or something with a zesty bounce, like Comic Sans italicized. Now, these are really ugly fonts, and they're difficult fonts to read. But at the end of the semester, students were given exams, and the students who'd been asked to read the more difficult fonts had actually done better on their exams, in a variety of subjects. And the reason is, the difficult font had slowed them down, forced them to work a bit harder, to think a bit more about what they were reading, to interpret it . . . and so they learned more." (Tim Harford, "How Frustration Can Make Us More Creative")

PRAYER

Creator God, please live within me and take all my chaos and indecisiveness and bring direction and confidence. Let all whom I lead see confidence. Take all my messy leadership and bring reason and care.

List some benefits and liabilities of chaos.

Think of someone who creates chaos.
How do you experience that person?

3

TWO KINDS OF COURAGE

"Be strong and of a good courage. Fear not, nor be afraid of them, for the LORD your God, it is He who goes with you. He will not fail you, nor forsake you."

Deuteronomy 31:6, MEV

"There are two kinds of courage, physical and moral, and he who would be a true leader must have both. Both are the products of the character-forming process, of the development of self-control, self-discipline, physical endurance, of knowledge of one's job and, therefore, of confidence. These qualities minimize fear and maximize sound judgment under pressure and—with some of that indispensable stuff called luck—often bring success from seemingly hopeless situations." (Matthew B. Ridgway, "Leadership")

PRAYER

God who sustains me, I am constantly faced with the challenge to remain courageous. Strengthen me so that I may meet the challenge and be resolute against all temptations.

Think of some people who are good in a crisis.
What are their characteristics?

—4—
TREATING PEOPLE WITH RESPECT AND DIGNITY

"God created humanity in God's own image,
in the divine image God created them,
male and female God created them."

Genesis 1:27, CEB

"A leader who treats his team members with respect and dignity can win the loyalty of subordinates literally for life. Throughout his entire career, George H. W. Bush was consistently kind to all those who worked with and for him. Most memorable were the countless little notes he would send to people who had gone out of their way for him, had received recognition of some sort for an accomplishment, had just done a good job, or had suffered some kind of personal tragedy or setback. He treated everyone— from White House groundskeepers to cabinet officers—the same way, asking about their families and their children (usually by name), asking how things were going for them generally, talking about the latest sports event of note. Virtually all who worked for him were considered part of a larger family, and no one ever forgot it . . . never underestimate the power of a kind word. Treating subordinates properly always pays dividends—and others notice. It doesn't mean being a soft touch." (Robert M. Gates, "It's Always about People," in *A Passion for Leadership—Lessons on Change and Reform from Fifty Years of Public Service*)

PRAYER

Dear God, you created each person in your divine image. Help me see that image in others. Help me to see worth and value in those whom you have placed in my care. Remind me of my responsibility to support them as your creation.

What happens to those people who never get the respect they deserve and need? How can you embody kindness with those you lead?

—5—
DEPENDABLE LEADING

"God in dependable love shows up on time,
shows me my enemies in ruin."

Psalm 59:10, The Message

"There are a number of reasons why the productive conversations in a meeting seemingly go nowhere. Attendees are often immediately running to another meeting where their attention shifts to a new set of issues. Or people leave the meeting without clarity about what was agreed upon. To make sure productivity doesn't slow after you walk out of the room, do two things after and in between meetings: Quickly send out clear and concise meeting notes and follow up on the commitments made. . . . Some managers are concerned that close follow-up might be interpreted as micromanaging. They don't want to be accused of not trusting people to perform. In reality, consistent follow-up is a necessary part of project leadership." (Paul Axtell, "Two Things to Do After Every Meeting")

PRAYER

God, you are always dependable despite my undependability. I can always rest upon your word and trust your reasons though I may not understand. Help me to be such a leader to those who depend on me.

What are the benefits, obstacles,
and limitations to being dependable?

What are the characteristics of
dependable leaders that you admire?

— 6 —
DARING TO DO OUR DUTY

"That's the whole story. Here now is my
final conclusion: Fear God and obey his
commands, for this is everyone's duty."

Ecclesiastes 12:13, NLT

"Neither let us be slandered from our duty by false accusations against us, nor frightened from it by menaces of destruction to the government, nor of dungeons to ourselves. Let us have faith that right makes might, and in that faith let us to the end dare to do our duty as we understand it." —Abraham Lincoln (Donald T. Phillips, *Lincoln on Leadership: Executive Strategies for Tough Times*)

PRAYER

God, be by my side this and every day. Be my strength, my rock, and leader of my soul. Help me to do my duty caring for those I lead and be resolute against all criticisms, doubts, and fears.

Why is the concept of duty so difficult for some people?
Who is someone you know who does their duty with grace?

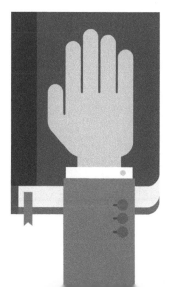

— 7 —
CLAIM THE RISKS
AS GIFTS FROM GOD

"Who knows but that you were brought
to the kingdom for a time like this?"

Esther 4:14, ISV

"Effective leaders develop a sense of purpose by pursuing goals that align with their personal values and advance the collective good. This allows them to look beyond the status quo to what is *possible* and gives them a compelling reason to take action despite personal fears and insecurities. Such leaders are seen as authentic and trustworthy because they are willing to take risks in the service of shared goals. By connecting others to a larger purpose, they inspire commitment, boost resolve, and help colleagues find deeper meaning in their work." (Herminia Ibarra, Robin Ely, and Deborah Kolb, "Women Rising: The Unseen Barriers")

PRAYER

God, you have made each of us with love and care, giving us a destiny of service. Help me see others as you see them.

How might God be using you in your
ministry context to lead God's people?

1

BEING A RELIABLE LEADER

"The Lord detests dishonest scales, but delights in an
accurate weight. When pride comes, so does shame,
but wisdom brings humility. Integrity guides the
virtuous, but dishonesty ruins the treacherous."

Proverbs 11:1-3, CEB

"For any leader, an important tool of leadership is the promise, a statement of
intended future action. Leaders are constantly making promises to their followers.
. . . Reliability in a leadership relationship means essentially that a leader keeps
his [or her] promises and commitments to other persons. Once followers start to
doubt a leader's reliability, the leadership relationship will begin to erode and with
it a leader's ability to lead. Reliability also implies honesty. . . . Politicians . . . and
countless corporate executives . . . have discovered, one of the quickest ways to
lose your power to lead is to be caught committing acts that are illegal, immoral, or
unethical." (Jeswald Salacuse, *Leading Leaders: How to Manage Smart, Talented,
Rich, and Powerful People*)

PRAYER

God, your word I do not doubt. Your ways, I do not doubt. Help me keep my word so
that I can reflect your will.

What are some promises you have made recently?
Think of a time when someone had to
depend on you keeping your word.

— 2 —
MAKING JUDGMENTS WITH INTEGRITY AND WISDOM

"Now faith is the substance of things hoped for,
the evidence of things not seen."

Hebrews 11:1, NKJV

"Judgment is hard to define. It is a fusion of your thinking, feelings, experience, imagination, and character. But five practical questions can improve your odds of making sound judgments, even when the data is incomplete or unclear, opinions are divided, and the answers are far from obvious. . . . How should the manager approach this situation? Not by following her gut instinct. Not by simply falling into line. Instead, she needs to systematically work through the five questions: What are the net consequences of all my options? What are my core obligations? What will work in the world as it is? Who are we? What can I live with?" (Joseph L. Badaracco, "How to Tackle Your Toughest Decisions")

PRAYER

God, give me the faith to move mountains; help me to discern the answers to questions placed before me. Knowing that my answers will change people's lives leaves me feeling unsure. Help others have faith in me.

What constitutes sound judgment? What can you live with?

— 3 —
COURAGE TO MAKE A DECISION

"But let him ask in faith, with no doubting, for the one who doubts is like a wave of the sea that is driven and tossed by the wind. For that person must not suppose that he will receive anything from the Lord; he is a double-minded man, unstable in all his ways."

James 1:6-8, ESV

"While an open mind is priceless, it is priceless only when its owner has the courage to make a final decision which closes the mind for action after the process of viewing all sides of the question has been completed. Failure to make a decision after due consideration of all the facts will quickly brand a man as unfit for a position of responsibility. Not all of your decisions will be correct. None of us is perfect. But if you get into the habit of making decisions, experience will develop your judgment to a point where it is better to be right fifty percent of the time and get something done, than it is to get nothing done because you fear to reach a decision." (H. W. Andrews, source unknown)

PRAYER

God, strengthen my resolve and bring me wisdom in deciding which path to take for myself and those I lead. Guard me from arrogance and selfishness in my choices. Let your light go before me, taking away all shadows of doubt.

How might you help strengthen
the resolve of those you lead?

—4—
MAKING THE HARD DECISIONS

"Desire without knowledge is not good, and one
who moves too hurriedly misses the way."

Proverbs 19:2, NRSV

A good leader has to make the hard call. You can build the justification, show the facts, let the person down easy, but in the end, someone is going to be upset. It's one thing to declare you are going to prioritize, but it's another to tell someone face-to-face that the project they've led for five years is going away. Doing that in a sensitive but firm way is what great leaders are made of, and it will inevitably have a cost. Here are some ways to improve your chances of success:

1. Build a solid case.
2. Keep the end goal and customer in mind.
3. Follow the process.

In behavioral economics they talk about the dynamic between your current self and your future self. Your current self might be assured of a decision, but your future self can be confronted with doubts that seem compelling in the moment. (Adapted from Alan Pentz, "Leadership Is About Hard Decisions")

PRAYER

God of all wisdom and understanding, before me today and each day are hard and difficult decisions that affect the lives of those I lead. Counsel me so that I can have the courage to make the decision and the peace that it is the right one.

Think of some tough decisions you've made.
What made them difficult?

5

ACTS OF KINDNESS
DEFINE A LEADER

"May the LORD reward your efforts! May your acts
of kindness be repaid fully by the LORD God of Israel,
from whom you have sought protection!"

Ruth 2:12, NET

"By definition, a leader is a trailblazer—someone who does things others don't do, often because they are the right things to do. These don't have to be heroic acts. Most likely, they are small, daily acts of kindness." Show kindness when someone is being disrespected at work. It may happen a lot, but it is never appropriate. Show kindness when someone needs your coaching, even if that person is not your employee. Show kindness by listening. You might learn something. Show kindness by demonstrating appreciation for those who possess great skill or potential. Show kindness by shutting down gossip and not gossiping yourself. Show kindness when someone needs relief from stress or is hurting. "Leaders set the example. Exercising your courage in small acts of kindness every day is one way to do that. Stop, notice those around you, and act in their best interest." (Adapted from Mary Jo Asmus, "Showing Courage in Small Acts of Kindness")

PRAYER

Loving God, you have been so gracious and kind to me when I am undeserving. Help me today to show that same care for those I lead.

When was the last time someone showed you kindness?

When was the last time you showed someone
in your care kindness? What happened?

— 6 —
BE PROACTIVE AS YOU CHARGE FORWARD

"Deborah said to Barak, 'Charge! This very day God has given you victory over Sisera. Isn't God marching before you?' Barak charged down the slopes of Mount Tabor, his ten companies following him."

Judges 4:14, The Message

"People commonly think being proactive means simply starting sooner rather than later, not procrastinating, or taking initiative to get work done. But it is far more than that. Your behavior is proactive when:

1. You choose it yourself rather than comply with external demands;
2. You execute strategically more than mindlessly;
3. You are future-focused rather than anchored in the present or past;
4. Your intention is to change something for the better, thus to create a better future.

Proactivity begins with recognizing that a current trajectory—your own, your team's, your company's, your country's—is not good enough, or downright bad, and deciding to make a course correction. More concretely, proactivity means solving or preventing problems and identifying and capturing opportunities, en route to a future that is better than if you had not changed course." (Thomas Bateman and Mike Crant, "Why Proactive Leadership Is Important")

PRAYER

Living God, incite me with passion and action. Stir my heart so I may move forward with courage and wisdom.

Think of some decisions you have ahead of you. How can you execute strategically and how can you demonstrate that you are future-focused?

How can you demonstrate your intention to change something for the better?

— 7 —
THE WAY FORWARD IN CLARITY

"You must inscribe on the stones all the
words of this law, making them clear."

Deuteronomy 27:8, NET

"Clarity in leadership is the ability to

- see through messes and contradictions;

- make things as clear as they can be and communicate that clarity (in other words, make things clear—but not artificially clear);

- see futures that others cannot see;

- find a viable direction in the midst of confusion; and

- see hope on the other side of trouble.

As volatility, uncertainty, complexity, and ambiguity increase, there will be many people wanting to be led out of the mess. . . . As the world gets more confusing, it will become harder to have legitimate clarity, to see through the mess to a better future. False clarity will abound. . . . The best leaders are seers, sensors, and listeners. They seek clarity from many sources, even as they hone their own inner clarity." (Bob Johansen, *Leaders Make the Future: Ten New Leadership Skills for an Uncertain World*)

PRAYER

Gracious God, the way is clear. The purpose is strong. I will follow where you lead, for I believe this is our path. Help me lead those in my care with purpose.

What messes have you cleaned up?
What did you learn? Who cleans up after you?

FLOURISH

1

ORIENT YOURSELF WITH GRATITUDE

"All this is for your benefit, so that the grace that is reaching more and more people may cause thanksgiving to overflow to the glory of God."

2 Corinthians 4:15, NIV

"After waking from a healthy and restful sleep session, prayer and meditation are crucial for orienting yourself toward the positive. What you focus on expands. Prayer and meditation facilitate intense gratitude for all that you have. Gratitude is having an abundance mindset. When you think abundantly, the world is your oyster. There is limitless opportunity and a possibility for you. People are magnets. When you're grateful for what you have, you will attract more of the positive and good. Gratitude is contagious. Gratitude may be the most important key to success. It has been called the mother of all virtues. If you start every morning putting yourself in a space of gratitude and clarity, you will attract the best the world has to offer, and not get distracted." (Benjamin P. Hardy, "8 Things Every Person Should Do Before 8 am")

PRAYER

Almighty God, I am thankful for all you have given me, even the gift of leading. Help me not fear the future but keep before me your steadfast loving-kindness.

List twenty-five things you are grateful for
and share some of them with your team.

1 _____
2 _____
3 _____
4 _____
5 _____
6 _____
7 _____
8 _____
9 _____
10 _____
12 _____
13 _____
14 _____
15 _____
16 _____
17 _____
18 _____
19 _____
20 _____
21 _____
22 _____
23 _____
24 _____
25 _____

2

QUIET TRANSPARENCY

"When pride comes, then comes disgrace,
but with humility comes wisdom."

Proverbs 11:2, NET

"Quiet transparency in leadership begins with humility. Leaders should be self-effacing and not self-promoting. Leaders must listen carefully. They should also be open. Why are you doing what you are doing? Why does it matter to you? More people will be interested in why leaders do what they do. . . . Leadership control is often illusory. Most top executives are surprised when they reach the top and learn that they have less power than they'd imagined. In the world of the future, control will rarely be possible. . . . Often the best leaders get little credit for the changes that they bring about." (Bob Johansen, *Leaders Make the Future: Ten New Leadership Skills for an Uncertain World*)

PRAYER

God, nothing is hidden from you. When I try to play power games, humble my spirit to realize that you are on my side always. Let those who follow me see a transparent person.

What tempts you to exert unhealthy pride?

What is the difference between healthy and unhealthy pride?

— 3 —

AFTER A VACATION, APPROACH YOUR TO–DO LIST THOUGHTFULLY

"Be careful to obey all these regulations I am giving you, so that it may always go well with you and your children after you, because you will be doing what is good and right in the eyes of the LORD your God."

Deuteronomy 12:28, NIV

Coming back from vacation can be painful. But you can do a few things to make the return easier. Use your first thirty minutes in the office to look through what's on your to-do list and make a plan for it. Keep in mind that what's most urgent now may not be what was most urgent before your time away. Check in with key people to discuss what you missed and what needs your attention. Thank anyone who covered for you and ask them what they need from you now. If you have to read all the emails that came in while you were away, start by scanning your inbox for key names—your boss's or a big client's—and read those first. And as you resume work, don't let the vacation glow fade. Take moments to remember the best experiences of your time away and use them to tap into the joy or calm you need to stay energized. (Adapted from Tristan Elizabeth Gribbin, "How to Minimize Stress Before, During, and After Your Vacation")

PRAYER

God of all, there is so much for me to do, and it seems so overwhelming. Guide my decisions so I will lead with wisdom and accomplish what is most important.

124

How do you set your priorities? your team's priorities?

125

4

FIVE BUILDING BLOCKS OF AGILITY

"But they who wait for the LORD shall renew their strength; they shall mount up with wings like eagles; they shall run and not be weary; they shall walk and not faint."

Isaiah 40:31, ESV

1. **Pause to move faster.** By pausing, leaders can create space for clear judgment, original thinking, and purposeful action.
2. **Embrace your ignorance.** Fresh ideas can come from anywhere, and listening—and thinking—from a place of not knowing is critical to encouraging the discovery of breakthrough ideas.
3. **Radically reframe the questions.** Asking yourself challenging questions may help unblock your existing mental model.
4. **Set direction, not destination.** Instead of telling your team to move from point A to point B, join them in a journey toward a vision of the future that sparks inspiration. Lead with purposeful vision, not just achievements. Ask, "How will we know we are successful beyond targets and metrics?" rather than, "What will we achieve?"
5. **Test your solutions—and yourself.** Quick, cheap failures can avert major, costly disasters. Think of yourself as a living laboratory to make leading change exciting instead of terrifying.

(Adapted from Johanne Lavoie and Jens Riese, "*Leaders*: It's OK to Not Know Everything")

PRAYER

Holy God, so much is expected that sometimes I feel overwhelmed. But I know you are faithful and will shelter me in your wings.

What questions do you need to reframe? In what direction are you leading? Where are you being tested?

127

— 5 —
MOVING FROM AGILE
TO TRANSFORMATIVE

"He gives strength to those who are tired; to the ones
who lack power, he gives renewed energy."

Isaiah 40:29, NET

"Disruptive times call for transformational leaders to let go and become more complex themselves to navigate effectively. Little attention has been paid to the cognitive and emotional load that dynamic change creates for leaders. It's an especially onerous burden, because the very nature of disruption means that leaders must steer their organizations into—and through—a fog of uncertainty. It's increasingly clear that to 'do' agile, you must 'be' agile. How do you do that? By growing more complex ourselves. To do that requires building a bigger inner self so complexity feels simpler and allows us to move with greater purpose, clarity, inner calm, and impact. Instead of getting frustrated with all the challenges or with ourselves and our habits, it pays to make the habit your friend." (Johanne Lavoie and Jens Riese, "Leaders: It's OK to Not Know Everything")

PRAYER

God, you share my heart and life in all things; strengthen me and renew my spirit for the seemingly impossible tasks ahead of me as a leader.

How do you recharge and keep yourself from burning out? Is your strategy for this successful?

— 6 —

MAKE IT EASIER FOR YOUR BOSS TO GIVE YOU NEGATIVE FEEDBACK

"He commanded them: 'Carry out your duties with respect for the Lord, with honesty, and with pure motives.'"

2 Chronicles 19:9, NET

It's hard to improve your skills when you don't know what to work on. If your boss isn't forthcoming with constructive feedback, try to make it easier for them. Start by giving yourself negative feedback, which will demonstrate that you're serious. Tell your boss something like, "I know that I tend to work quickly and sometimes overlook important details. I'd like to get better at that. Do you have any thoughts on how I could do it?" You could also tell your manager that you want to improve in three areas this year and that you'd like their feedback on what the areas should be. Ask, "Would you please help me keep this commitment I've made to myself?" That way, they can think of their feedback as helping you make good on a promise, not as hurting your feelings. (Adapted from Deborah Grayson Riegel, "How to Solicit Negative Feedback When Your Manager Doesn't Want to Give It")

PRAYER

God of truth, I know you see and understand me, and I cannot hide. You know me better than I know myself. Speak to me that I may hear truth. Speak through others so I may hear your voice. Now, help me today to be a person who can speak truth to those I lead.

What constructive feedback do you need to hear?

7

THE CORNERSTONE OF LEADERSHIP

"Now therefore revere the LORD, and serve him in
sincerity and in faithfulness; put away the gods
that your ancestors served beyond the River
and in Egypt, and serve the LORD."

Joshua 24:14, NRSV

"In order to be a leader a man [or woman] must have followers. And to have followers, a man [or woman] must have their confidence. Hence the supreme quality of a leader is unquestionably integrity. Without it, no real success is possible, no matter whether it is on a section gang, on a football field, in an army, or in an office. If a man's [or woman's] associates find him [or her] guilty of phoniness, if they find that he [or she] lacks forthright integrity, he [or she] will fail. His [or her] teachings and actions must square with each other. The first great need, therefore, is integrity and high purpose." (Dwight D. Eisenhower, *The Best of Bits & Pieces*)

PRAYER

God, I will be tested today. My character will be challenged. Help me to hold fast to my integrity and serve you faithfully.

Do you always keep your word?
How do you demonstrate your integrity?

1
SEVEN WAYS TO SHOW APPRECIATION

"It will not be so among you; but whoever wishes to be great among you must be your servant."

Matthew 20:26, NRSV

- Remind employees often that what they do is important.
- Criticize in private and focus on specifics.
- Make clear that if they don't understand the boss's guidance or decisions, they have a responsibility to seek clarification.
- Avoid setting up task forces or committees unless there is a reasonable certainty they will come up with useful recommendations.
- Establish specific goals and milestones for tasks. A good leader must accept responsibility if it proves a dead end or a mistake.
- Listen to their practical concerns.
- Publicly praise employees at every level as often as possible when it is deserved.

(Adapted from Robert M. Gates, *A Passion for Leadership: Lessons on Change and Reform from Fifty Years of Public Service*)

PRAYER

God, it is not about me but about others. Help me to be the servant leader who cares and shows appreciation to others. Keep my heart pure.

To whom do you need to show greater appreciation?

2

ESTABLISHING TRUST IN A TEAM

"They rose early in the morning and went out into the wilderness of Tekoa; and as they went out, Jehoshaphat stood and said, Listen to me, O Judah and inhabitants of Jerusalem! Believe in the LORD your God and you will be established; believe his prophets."

2 Chronicles 20:20, NRSV

"Trust lies at the heart of a functioning, cohesive team. Without it, teamwork is all but impossible. Unfortunately, the word *trust* is used—and misused—so often that it has lost some of its impact and begins to sound like motherhood and apple pie. That is why it is important to be very specific about what is meant by trust. In the context of building a team, trust is the confidence among team members that their peers' intentions are good, and that there is no reason to be protective or careful around the group. In essence, teammates must get comfortable being vulnerable with one another." (Patrick Lencioni, *The Five Dysfunctions of a Team*)

PRAYER

God, you above all are most trustworthy. Strengthen my trust in you. Help me follow where you lead and help me to lead those you have placed in my care so I may earn their trust.

Who do you trust? What makes a person trustworthy?
Are you trustworthy?

3

SOLITUDE TO FOCUS

"Be still, and know that I am God: I will be exalted among the heathen, I will be exalted in the earth."

Psalm 46:10, KJV

"There is no silver bullet to solving the complex problems ushered in by the information age. But there are some good places to start, and one of them is counterintuitive: solitude. Having the discipline to step back from the noise of the world is essential to staying focused. This is even more important in a highly politicized society that constantly incites our emotions, causing the cognitive effects of distractions to linger. . . . The ability to focus is a competitive advantage in the world today. Here are some thoughts on how to stay focused at work:

- Build periods of solitude into your schedule.
- Analyze where your time is best spent.
- Starve your distractions.
- Don't be too busy to learn how to be less busy.
- Create a 'stop doing' list."

(Mike Erwin, "In a Distracted World, Solitude Is a Competitive Advantage")

PRAYER

God of the quiet and holy, I pause in my hurry and life of noise and turn to you. I still my mind and listen with my soul. Speak words of assurance and comfort. Open my mind to wise counsel so I may lead with wisdom.

What are some complex problems that need your attention?

How are you addressing them?

Who can help you?

4

TO GROW AND EVOLVE IN THE MIDST OF FLUX

"[God] went in the way before you to search
out a place for you to pitch your tents, to show
you the way you should go, in the fire by night
and in the cloud by day."

Deuteronomy 1:33, NKJV

"All life lives off-balance in a world that is open to change. And all of life is self-organizing. We do not have to fear disequilibrium, nor do we have to approach change so fearfully. Instead, we can realize that, like all life, we know how to grow and evolve in the midst of constant flux. There is a path through change that leads to greater independence and resiliency. We dance along this path by maintaining a coherent identity and by honoring everybody's need for self-determination." (Margaret Wheatley, *Leadership and the New Science: Discovering Order in a Chaotic World*)

PRAYER

God, it seems there is nothing that is not changing. But you never change. You are my constant and my strength. Help me stand strong before those you have placed in my care.

When was the last time you were caught off-balance? Why? What happened? Would you do anything differently?

—5—
LEADING WITH
ETHICAL EXCELLENCE

"Let every detail in your lives—words, actions,

whatever—be done in the name of the Master, Jesus,

thanking God the Father every step of the way."

Colossians 3:17, The Message

"Ethical thinkers are catalysts. The moral viewpoint, however gently added to a situation, has an uncanny way of stimulating the process. Positions that were uncertain take on a new sharpness. Attitudes that were grudgingly congruent can suddenly diverge. People who once whispered can begin to shout. That can be unnerving. As the ethical battle rages, all sorts of stench can erupt—and all sorts of sludge can precipitate to the bottom. But it can also be exhilarating. There is nothing more satisfying than to see apathy overcome, stagnation broken, and decisions made that absolutely transform their surroundings for the better. And there is nothing more comforting than to feel some assurance that such decisions, when arrived at through ethical processes, constitute the highest level of right we can reach." (Rushworth M. Kidder, *How Good People Make Tough Choices: Resolving the Dilemmas of Ethical Living*)

PRAYER

God of all that is right and pure, examine me for impurities. Show and lead me to the moral high ground of truth.

Reflect on a time when you took the moral high ground.
What happened? How did you avoid being or appearing
to be moralistic and judgmental?

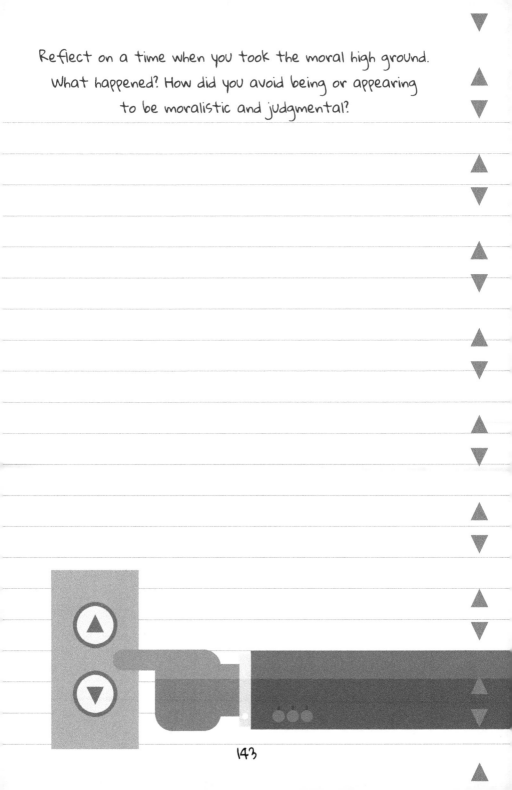

— 6 —
REPUTATION

"A good name is to be chosen rather than great wealth, good favor more than silver or gold. The rich and the poor meet together; the LORD is the Creator of them both. A shrewd person sees danger and hides himself, but the naive keep right on going and suffer for it. The reward for humility and fearing the LORD is riches and honor and life."

Proverbs 22:1-4, NET

"We live in an age where maintaining an organization's reputation and brand management is a constant challenge. Of the many ways corporate reputations are made and lost, few are more important than the quality of their leaders. Consumers are negatively influenced by headlines of errant and unethical behavior and positively influenced by lists of most-admired practices. . . . In a world of choices, they will provide feedback by remaining loyal to a brand or by choosing a competitor for essentially the same product. They often share their thoughts and feelings among the members of their social networks with messages and postings that seem to never fade from the Internet." (Jack Phillips, Patricia Pulliam Phillips, and Rebecca L. Ray, *Measuring Leadership Development: Quantify Your Program's Impact and ROI on Organizational Performance*)

PRAYER

God, your ways are beyond our ways and we know you never fail us. Teach me to guard my integrity, actions, and words. Strengthen how others will know I am a person of integrity.

144

What words do people use when describing you?
Are they on target?

— 7 —
MULTIPLYING PEOPLE POTENTIAL

"With pride comes only contention,
but wisdom is with the well-advised."

Proverbs 13:10, NET

"Some leaders drain all the intelligence and capability out of their teams. Because they need to be the smartest, most capable person in the room, these managers often shut down the smarts of others, ultimately stifling the flow of ideas. . . . You know these people, because you've worked for and with them. These leaders—we call them 'diminishers'—underutilize people and leave creativity and talent on the table. . . . At the other extreme are leaders who, as capable as they are, care less about flaunting their own IQs and more about fostering a culture of intelligence in their organizations. . . . Under the leadership of these 'multipliers,' employees don't feel smarter, they become smarter." (Liz Wiseman and Greg McKeown, "Managing Yourself: Bringing Out the Best in Your People")

PRAYER

Creator of all knowledge, humble my spirit to be a servant. Help me to use my wisdom and insight for the good beyond my own recognition. I lift up those whom I lead that they will flourish.

Do you have to be the smartest person in the room?
How do you handle disagreement over the facts?

— 1 —
FALLING IN LOVE
WITH LEADING

"Above all, show sincere love to each other, because love
brings about the forgiveness of many sins."

1 Peter 4:8, CEB

"To become the best leader you can be, you have to fall in love with the work you are
doing and with the reason you are doing it. You have to fall in love with leading and
the purpose you are serving. . . . We're talking about the kind of love that Stephen
J. Dubner and Steven D. Levitt, authors of the bestselling book *Freakonomics*, write
about when they say, 'When it comes to choosing a life path, you should do what you
love—because if you don't love it, you are unlikely to work hard enough to get very
good.' We're talking about the same kind of love people feel when they have a passion
for something, when they want to be the very best at something." (James M. Kouzes
and Barry Z. Posner, *The Truth About Leadership: The No-Fads, Heart-of-the-Matter
Facts You Need to Know*)

PRAYER

God who loves me deeply, lighten my heart to feel the care and passion of my job
and leadership responsibility. Make every day a new day of discovery and growth.
Fuel my heart with a caring love for those I lead.

What parts of your job do you love?
What parts of the job do those you lead love?

149

— 2 —
GIVE THANKS FOR THESE PEOPLE

"Tell the innocent it will go well with them, for they
will be rewarded for what they have done."

Isaiah 3:10, NET

- The Inspirational Leader: Because their vision and execution inspire the team to bring their best.
- The Curiosity Royalty: These people are always asking questions, itching to improve processes, attending workshops, and then briefing the team on the latest know-how. They are instrumental players in the success and innovation the team delivers.
- The Core Team: These people deserve a note of appreciation for the camaraderie, support, and knowledge they provide year-round.
- The Connector: This person knows people and brings them together to solve problems and move mountains.
- The Grounder: This person will raise an eyebrow when you pitch what you think is a revolutionary plan to reinvent, rejuvenate, and transform the world. If not for Grounders, many of us would be trapped in the clouds of possibility.
- The Lunch Group: These are the coworkers you naturally gravitate toward, who share your jokes, have your back, and celebrate your successes with a fun lunch out.

(Adapted from David Sturt and Todd Nordstrom, "The 6 People at Work to Thank Before Thanksgiving, And After")

PRAYER

God of all blessings and goodness, I bow my head in thanksgiving and gratitude for all you have given me in this position. Thank you for their faithful work.

Identify your Inspirational Leaders, Curiosity Royalty,
Core Team, Connectors, Grounders, and Lunch Group.

Inspirational Leaders   Curiosity Royalty

                        Core Team

Connectors, Grounders   Lunch Group

—3—
LEADING AUTONOMY FOR PERFORMANCE AND SATISFACTION

"Do not be afraid, little flock, for it is your
Father's good pleasure to give you the kingdom."

Luke 12:32, MEV

"A sense of autonomy has a powerful effect on individual performance and attitude. According to a cluster of recent behavioral science studies, autonomous motivation promotes greater conceptual understanding, better grades, enhanced persistence at school and in sporting activities, higher productivity, less burnout, and greater levels of psychological well-being." (Daniel H. Pink, *Drive: The Surprising Truth About What Motivates Us*)

PRAYER

God of all, help me believe in my team and help them do their best. Help them know that you are always with them.

On a scale of one to ten (one is low and ten is high),
how much are you a micromanager? How do you respond
to being micromanaged?

4

SOUL FORTITUDE

"Bless the Lord, O my soul, and all that is
within me, bless his holy name."

Psalm 103:1, NRSV

"I had prepared myself to face it, as all men [and women] must steel their souls to face new and unknown dangers. But in the darkness after you have gone to bed, when you are not the commander with stars on your shoulders, but just one man [or woman], alone with your God in the dark, your thoughts inevitably turn inward, and out of whatever resources of the spirit you possess, you prepare yourself as best you may for whatever tests may lie ahead." (Charles W. Arnade, *Soldier: The Memoirs of Matthew B. Ridgway*)

PRAYER

Dear Blessed Savior, you see that I don't have all the answers. I am sometimes unsure and fearful that my decisions will hurt others and fail before the world. Be with me when I feel alone.

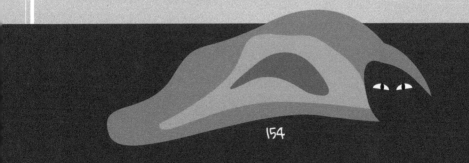

What do you fear most about being a leader?

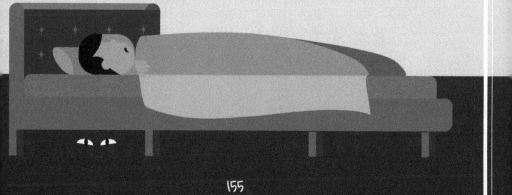

— 5 —

ETHICAL FITNESS

"As for you, brothers and sisters,
never tire of doing what is good."

2 Thessalonians 3:13, NIV

"In a sense, then, ethical fitness is like character—which, we've been told, is what you are in the dark, when no one's looking. . . . In the hurly-burly of today's world, however, such moments are few. Far more common are tests of ethical fitness that happen when everyone's watching, the reward is significant, and time is short. Ethical fitness is indeed private and personal. But it's also public and social. . . . Yes, character is what you are in the dark. But it's more. It has a social as well as a personal aspect. First, it's what you let others know you to be—the way you communicate to others an openness to ethical concern, a willingness to engage tough moral issues, an invitation to challenge your actions by your values. Second, ethical fitness doesn't exist in a personal vacuum. Third, ethical fitness benefits mightily from an organizational culture . . . the institution applauds and rewards such behavior." (Rushworth M. Kidder, *How Good People Make Tough Choices*)

PRAYER

Creator of heaven, earth, and the universe, help me to be, to think, to act what is right and good because it is right and good. Make me truthful, honest, and honorable in all things.

156

How does your leadership culture reflect your ethics and values? What would those you lead say?

6
UNDERSTANDING PEOPLE

"And he said to them, 'Pay attention to what you hear: with the measure you use, it will be measured to you, and still more will be added to you.'"

Mark 4:24, ESV

"Management expert Ken Blanchard examined [Coach John] Wooden's leadership techniques and found that his understanding of group dynamics was fundamental to his success. 'What's fascinating about basketball is a wonderful metaphor for life, for organizations, for businesses. His basic philosophy is that none of us is as good as all of us. Basketball's a sport in which you might be good, but you can't win by yourself. A star player can't win a championship alone; he has to get a cast of characters around him who really play well with him.' By encouraging his athletes to push one another in positive ways toward a common goal, rather than just focusing on one or two stars, Wooden was able to foster trust and chemistry among his entire roster. The result was a culture of self-motivation that continued to attract players who shared the same value." (Don Yaeger, "John Wooden's Legacy Is a How-To Guide for a Successful Life")

PRAYER

God who understands me better than myself, help me to truly know those who follow me. As you value me, allow me to value those you put into my care.

What motivates you and helps you motivate others?

you got this!

GOOD JOB!

Way to go!

7

LISTEN AND FLOURISH

*"Let the wise listen and add to their learning,
and let the discerning get guidance."*

Proverbs 1:5, NIV

"General Otis made an impression on me that day. From then on, I carried a similar reminder to myself about being a good listener. As I progressed during my own career, I added two other attributes that I consider essential in a leader: understanding how to amplify and developing a genuine instinct to be inclusive. I describe the interaction of the three instincts this way:

Listen to learn. *Listen* to make it clear to those who follow that you value their insights, their judgments, and their advice.

Amplify to establish expectations. *Amplify* the best ideas, the best recommendations, the best practices, and do it in a manner that encourages teamwork at every level of the organization.

Include to empower. Go wide and deep in *including* members of the organization to share knowledge, to create a common understanding of problems, and to encourage ownership of solutions."

(Martin E. Dempsey, "Leadership Instincts: Listen, Amplify, Include")

PRAYER

God, I await your words of wisdom and guidance. You know today and tomorrow. Humble my heart to truly hear what others say and to gain further wisdom.

How often do you take time to listen to your staff?
What are three things you've learned from them recently?

—1—
FLOURISHING LEADERS TEACH

"Let the word of Christ dwell in you richly, teaching
and admonishing one another in all wisdom,
singing psalms and hymns and spiritual songs, with
thankfulness in your hearts to God."

Colossians 3:16, ESV

"Our experiences both with red wagons and the whole field trip strategy led me to an important conclusion—which has since become a key Santa leadership principle: *The more employees understand about how the business works, the more likely they are to accept and support change.* For us, teaching 'the business' of the business has been good business. It's given the elves and reindeer additional opportunities and it's produced greater workshop-wide acceptance, support, and understanding of the need for change. Most importantly, it's made them feel like true 'partners' in the running of our North Pole operation . . . because THEY ARE!" (Eric Harvey, *The Leadership Secrets of Santa Claus: How to Get Big Things Done in YOUR Workshop*)

PRAYER

Teacher, open my ears for your voice of wisdom. Open my heart for your spirit of humility. Guide me so I may instruct those I lead with both wisdom and humility.

In what areas are you qualified to teach?

What do your team members need to learn from you?

—2—
RESILIENT LEADERS FAIL

"He gives power to the faint,
and strengthens the powerless."

Isaiah 40:29, NRSV

"The first step toward developing resilience is challenging the idea that we can control everything. Rather than beat ourselves up for the disappointments and negative outcomes we inevitably experience at work (or elsewhere), we can learn to practice acceptance of ourselves and of our situations, whether good or bad. In so doing, we give ourselves the gift of mental space—and in this space we can learn to realize that difficult experiences and setbacks are actually opportunities for learning and growth." (Charlotte Lieberman, "How to Never Feel Stressed at Work Again")

PRAYER

God, I sometimes think I have control, but when I face reality, I know it is an illusion. Only you can truly see truth, and so I lean on you for that strength and forgiveness for my failures. Help me to learn from those setbacks.

How is it with your soul? How is the morale of your team?

— 3 —
MAKING YESTERDAY PERFECT

"The law of the LORD is perfect,
converting the soul: the testimony of the
LORD is sure, making wise the simple."

Psalm 19:7, KJV

"Making Yesterday Perfect is still another form of inability to cope effectively with external change. The Making Yesterday Perfect leader is often zealous in making change, even demonstrating great 'progress,' but always in terms of the old paradigm. Such a leader is a great 'fixer' and often has elaborate inspection and control systems to measure processes and performance against precise standards. Making Yesterday Perfect is a particularly treacherous type of resistance to change within an organization, because it is so easy to appear to be engaged in making changes and 'modernization'; there can be a very high level of activity; and specific actions, usually incremental, are generally easy to defend because the context is stable and therefore risk invariably appears to be low." (Gordon R. Sullivan and Michael V. Harper, *Hope Is Not a Method: What Business Leaders Can Learn from America's Army*)

PRAYER

God who is perfect yesterday, today, and tomorrow, give me courage for change and to take the necessary risks. Give me the wisdom to make the right decisions.

When was the last time you tried something new?
How do you introduce change as a leader?

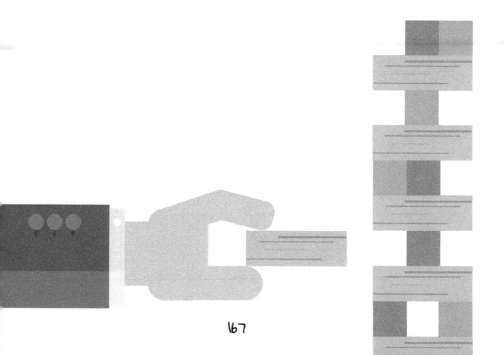

—4—
OUR LEADER LEGACY

"Remember the long road on which the Lord your God led you during these forty years in the desert so he could humble you, testing you to find out what was in your heart: whether you would keep his commandments or not."

Deuteronomy 8:2, CEB

"People sometimes ask me how I want to be remembered. . . . But when the day comes, I hope people will say that I did the best with what I was given, tried to make my parents proud, served my country with all the energy I had, and took a strong stand on the side of freedom. Perhaps some will also say that I helped teach a generation of older women to stand tall and young women not to be afraid to interrupt." (Madeleine Albright, *Madam Secretary: A Memoir*)

PRAYER

God, do not forget me in my confusion, failures, and weaknesses. Help me to do my best and be counted as a person of integrity and humility. When someday I stand before you, I yearn to hear you say: "Well done, good and faithful servant."

What do you want to be remembered for?

—5—
THE LEGACY OF MENTORSHIP

"When they hear about your great reputation and your
ability to accomplish mighty deeds, they will come and
direct their prayers toward this temple."

1 Kings 8:42, NET

"Four-time World Series winner Joe Torre had a similar experience, finding himself on the receiving end of some powerful mentorship: 'I had recently started managing the Yankees and was sitting in my office one day, when suddenly a man walked through with no warning, causing me to jump to my feet. *What in the world was Coach Wooden doing in my office?* Of course, I knew him by reputation and knew the domination that UCLA had enjoyed during the 1960s and 1970s, but I never met the man. Now here he was, looking at me in the eye and saying, "I wanted to meet you because I like you, and I admire the way your teams play." I could barely stutter out my thanks before a parade of players started knocking on my door because they had seen Coach on his way up to my office and they all wanted to meet him, too.'" (Don Yaeger, "John Wooden's Legacy Is a How-To Guide for a Successful Life")

PRAYER

God, mentor me so that I may be pleasing in your sight. Shape and direct me to fulfill my promise as a leader. Now, give me the wisdom and humility to do the same to those you have placed in my care.

Who are you mentoring? Who mentors you?

GROWTH

6

DREAMING OF POSSIBILITIES AND POTENTIAL

"At Gibeon the LORD appeared to Solomon in a dream by night, and God said, 'Ask what I shall give you.'"

1 Kings 3:5, ESV

"Dreams always come from behind you, not right between your eyes. It sneaks up on you. But when you have a dream, it doesn't often come at you screaming in your face, 'This is who you are, this is what you must be for the rest of your life.' Sometimes a dream almost whispers. And I've always said to my kids, the hardest thing to listen to—your instincts, your human personal intuition—always whispers; it never shouts. Very hard to hear. So, you have to every day of your lives be ready to hear what whispers in your ear; it very rarely shouts. And if you can listen to the whisper, and if it tickles your heart, and it's something you think you want to do for the rest of your life, then that is going to be what you do for the rest of your life, and we will benefit from everything you do." (Steven Spielberg, Harvard Commencement Speech)

PRAYER

God, you have a purpose for my life, and you see my destiny and dreams of what I want to achieve and be. Help me make the dreams of those I lead become reality.

What is your big dream?
What is the first step toward realizing it?

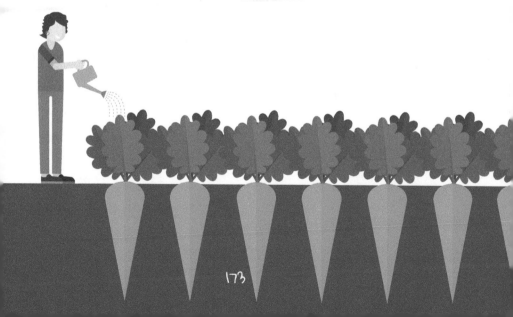

—7—
WHAT'S NEXT?

"I'm sure about this: the one who started a
good work in you will stay with you to complete
the job by the day of Christ Jesus."

Philippians 1:6, CEB

Want to be a better leader, more inspiring leader, be more productive, or take more risks? Then ask yourself two questions. First, do you really want to do better? Presumably the answer is "yes," but if you're looking to improve because, say, your boss wants you to, be honest about that. Change will happen only if you're committed to it. Second, are you willing to feel the discomfort of trying things that don't work right away? Learning anything new is inherently uncomfortable, so be prepared to feel a little awkward. You will make mistakes. You may feel embarrassed or ashamed, especially if you are used to succeeding. But if you remain committed through all of that, you will get better. (Adapted from Peter Bregman, "If You Want to Get Better at Something, Ask Yourself These Two Questions")

PRAYER

Dear God of my life, help me be the leader you intend, and help me join with you to accomplish your goals.

What is your next step?

How can you help others take their next steps?

SOURCES

Addison, John. "Leadership Lessons I Learned from My Family." *Success Magazine,* November 7, 2016, https://www.success.com/john-addison-leadership-lessons-i-learned-from-my-family/.

Albright, Madeleine. *Madam Secretary: A Memoir.* New York: Harper Perennial, 2013, p. 512.

Andrews, H. W. Source Unknown.

Arnade, Charles W. *Soldier: The Memoirs of Matthew B. Ridgway.* Andesite Press, 2017.

Asmus, Mary Jo. "How Small Acts of Kindness Show Courage—And Leadership," May 8, 2018, https://www.aspire-cs.com/showing-courage-in-small-acts-of-kindness/.

Axtell, Paul. "Two Things to Do After Every Meeting." *Harvard Business Review*, November 26, 2015, https://hbr.org/2015/11/two-things-to-do-after-every-meeting.

Badaracco, Joseph L. "How to Tackle Your Toughest Decisions." *Harvard Business Review*, September 2016, https://hbr.org/2016/09/how-to-tackle-your-toughest-decisions.

Badaracco, Joseph L. "Timeless Advice for Making a Hard Choice." *Harvard Business Review*, August 25, 2016, https://hbr.org/2016/08/timeless-advice-for-making-a-hard-choice.

Bateman, Thomas, and Mike Crant. "Why Proactive Leadership Is Important," July 18, 2018, http://theconversation.com/why-proactive-leadership-is-important-or-how-congress-could-have-prevented-trumps-helsinki-fiasco-100145.

Bennis, Warren. *On Becoming a Leader.* New York: Basic Books, 2009, p. 134.

Biddle, Matthew. "Many Don't See Women as Leaders at Work," August 18, 2018, https://www.futurity.org/women-workplaces-gender-equality-1830972/.

Blitchington, Peter, and Robert Cruise. *Understanding Your Temperament: A Self-Analysis with a Christian Viewpoint.* Berrien Springs, MI: Andrews University Press, 1979.

Bossidy, Larry, and Ram Charan. *Execution: The Discipline of Getting Things Done.* New York: Currency, 2009, p. 141.

Bradberry, Travis. "Here's Why Your Attitude Is More Important Than Your Intelligence," August 9, 2017, https://www.weforum.org/agenda/2017/08/heres-why-your-attitude-is-more-important-than-your-intelligence/.

Bregman, Peter. "How to Lead When You're Feeling Afraid." *Harvard Business Review*, June 13, 2018, https://hbr.org/2018/06/how-to-lead-when-youre-feeling-afraid.

Bregman, Peter. "If You Want to Get Better at Something, Ask Yourself These Two Questions." *Harvard Business Review*, November 9, 2018, https://hbr.org/2018/11/if-you-want-to-get-better-at-something-ask-yourself-these-two-questions?utm_medium=email&utm_source=newsletter_daily&utm_campaign=mtod_not_activesubs&referral=00203&deliveryName=DM22579.

Brooks, Donna, and Lynn Brooks. *Ten Secrets of Successful Leaders: The Strategies, Skills, and Knowledge Leaders at Every Level Need to Succeed*. New York: McGraw-Hill, 2005, pp. 46, 55.

Buckingham, Marcus. "What Great Managers Do." *Harvard Business Review*, March 2005, https://hbr.org/2005/03/what-great-managers-do.

Carucci, Ron. "Organizations Can't Change If Leaders Can't Change with Them." *Harvard Business Review*, October 24, 2016, https://hbr.org/2016/10/organizations-cant-change-if-leaders-cant-change-with-them.

Chamorro-Premuzic, Tomas. "How to Work for a Boss Who Lacks Self-Awareness." *Harvard Business Review*, April 3, 2018, https://hbr.org/2018/04/how-to-work-for-a-boss-who-lacks-self-awareness.

Collins, Jim. *How the Mighty Fall: And Why Some Companies Never Give In*. New York: HarperCollins, 2009, p. 123.

Dempsey, Martin E. "Leadership Instincts: Listen, Amplify, Include," LinkedIn, August 25, 2017, https://www.linkedin.com/pulse/leadership-instincts-listen-amplify-include-general-martin-e-dempsey/.

Deneen, Sally. "Women Who Leaned In," in *Success Magazine*, "What Achievers Read," Success Media, p. 67.

Eisenhower, Dwight D. *The Best of Bits & Pieces*. Economics Press, 1994, p. 4.

Erwin, Mike. "In a Distracted World, Solitude Is a Competitive Advantage." *Harvard Business Review*, October 19, 2017, https://hbr.org/2017/10/in-a-distracted-world-solitude-is-a-competitive-advantage.

Gates, Robert M. *A Passion for Leadership: Lessons on Change and Reform from Fifty Years of Public Service*. New York: Vintage, 2017, pp. 102–103, 107.

Goleman, Daniel, Richard Boyatzis, and Annie McKee. *Primal Leadership: Unleashing the Power of Emotional Intelligence*. Brighton, MA: Harvard Business Review Press, 2002, pp. 3, 7–8.

Grayson Riegel, Deborah. "How to Solicit Negative Feedback When Your Manager Doesn't Want to Give It." *Harvard Business Review*, March 5, 2018, https://hbr.org/2018/03/how-to-solicit-negative-feedback-when-your-manager-doesnt-want-to-give-it.

Gribbin, Tristan Elizabeth. "How to Minimize Stress Before, During, and After Your Vacation." *Harvard Business Review*, September 6, 2018, https://hbr.org/2018/09/how-to-minimize-stress-before-during-and-after-your-vacation.

Hardy, Benjamin P. "8 Things Every Person Should Do Before 8 am." *Ladders*, December 28, 2018, https://www.theladders.com/career-advice/8-things-every-person-should-do-before-8-am.

Harford, Tim. "How Frustration Can Make Us More Creative." http://www.ted.com/talks/tim_harford_how_messy_problems_can_inspire_creativity?utm_source=newsletter_weekly_2016-01-16&utm_campaign=newsletter_weekly&utm_medium=email&utm_content=bottom_left_button.

Harkavy, Daniel. *Becoming a Coaching Leader: A Proven System of Building Your Team of Champions*. New York: Harper Collins Leadership, 2010. pp. 19–23.

Harvey, Eric. *The Leadership Secrets of Santa Claus: How to Get Big Things Done in YOUR Workshop*. Naperville, IL: Simple Truths, 2015, pp. 22–23, 48–49.

Hougaard, Rasmus, and Jacqueline Carter. "Ego Is the Enemy of Good Leadership." *Harvard Business Review*, November 6, 2018, https://hbr.org/2018/11/ego-is-the-enemy-of-good-leadership.

Hunter, James C. *The Servant: A Simple Story about the True Essence of Leadership*. New York: Crown Business, 2000.

Ibarra, Herminia, Robin Ely, and Deborah Kolb. "Women Rising: The Unseen Barriers." *Harvard Business Review*, September 2013, https://hbr.org/2013/09/women-rising-the-unseen-barriers.

Johansen, Bob. *Leaders Make the Future: Ten New Leadership Skills for an Uncertain World*. Oakland, CA: Berrett-Koehler Publishers, 2012, p. 46, 127–128.

"John Kerry on Leadership, Compromise, and Change." *Harvard Business Review*, October 16, 2018, https://hbr.org/ideacast/2018/10/john-kerry-on-leadership-compromise-and-change.

Kaltman, Al. *Cigars, Whiskey, and Winning: Leadership Lessons from General Ulysses S. Grant*. Upper Saddle River, NJ: Prentice Hall, 2000, p. 112.

Kearns Goodwin, Doris. "Lincoln and the Art of Transformative Leadership." *Harvard Business Review*, September–October 2018, https://hbr.org/2018/09/lincoln-and-the-art-of-transformative-leadership.

Kidder, Rushworth M. *How Good People Make Tough Choices: Resolving the Dilemmas of Ethical Living*. Wichita, KS: Fireside, 1996, pp. 53–54, 209–210.

Kouzes, James M., and Barry Z. Posner. *The Truth About Leadership: The No-Fads, Heart-of-the-Matter Facts You Need to Know*. San Francisco: Jossey-Bass, 2010, pp. 145–146.

Lavoie, Johanne, and Jens Riese. "Leaders: It's OK to Not Know Everything," July 2, 2018, https://www.mckinsey.com/business-functions/organization/our-insights/the-organization-blog/leaders-its-ok-to-not-know-everything.

Lencioni, Patrick. *The Five Dysfunctions of a Team: A Leadership Fable*. San Francisco: Jossey-Bass, 2002, pp. 212–213.

Lieberman, Charlotte. "How to Never Feel Stressed at Work Again," May 13, 2014, https://greatist.com/happiness/how-to-never-feel-stressed-at-work-again.

Lynch, Rick. *Adapt or Die: Leadership Principles from an American General*. Grand Rapids, MI: Baker Books, 2013, p. 128.

McClelland, David C., and David H. Burnham, "Power Is the Great Motivator." *Harvard Business Review*, January 2003, https://hbr.org/2003/01/power-is-the-great-motivator.

Pentz, Alan. "Leadership Is About Hard Decisions," February 21, 2018, https://www.govexec.com/excellence/nextgen-strategist/2018/02/leadership-about-hard-decisions/146111/.

Phillips, Donald T. *Lincoln on Leadership: Executive Strategies for Tough Times*. New York: Warner Books Inc., 1993, p. 65.

Phillips, Jack, Patricia Pulliam Phillips, and Rebecca L. Ray. *Measuring Leadership Development: Quantify Your Program's Impact and ROI on Organizational Performance*. New York: McGraw-Hill Education, 2012, pp. 6–7.

Pink, Daniel H. *Drive: The Surprising Truth About What Motivates Us*. New York: Riverhead Books, 2009.

Powell, Colin. *It Worked for Me: In Life and Leadership*. New York: Harper Perennial, 2014, pp. 46-47.

Poynter Institute. *The Kennedys: America's Front-Page Family*. Kansas City, MO: Andrews McMeel Publishing, 2009, p. 112.

Ridgway, Matthew B. "Leadership." *Military Review* (October 1966): np.

Roosevelt, Theodore. *Theodore Roosevelt: An Autobiography*. Hollywood, FL: Simon and Brown, 2016.

Ryan, John. Center for Creative Leadership. https://www.ccl.org/people/john-ryan/.

Salacuse, Jeswald. *Leading Leaders: How to Manage Smart, Talented, Rich, and Powerful People*. New York: AMACOM, 2005, pp 31–32.

Shih, Clara. "10 Powerful Quotes from Female Leaders on International Women's Day." *Forbes*, March 8, 2018, https://www.forbes.com/sites/forbes-summit-talks/2018/03/08/10-powerful-quotes-from-female-leaders-on-international-womens-day/#19b8da503f0f.

Sinek, Simon. *Start with Why: How Great Leaders Inspire Everyone to Take Action*. New York: Portfolio, 2011, p. 84.

Spielberg, Steven. Commencement speech. Harvard University. May 26, 2016.

Sturt, David, and Todd Nordstrom. "The 6 People at Work to Thank Before Thanksgiving, And After." *Forbes*, November 20, 2015, https://www.forbes.com/sites/davidsturt/2015/11/20/the-6-people-at-work-to-thank-before-thanksgiving-and-after/#4d2a598a494a.

Sullivan, Gordon R., and Michael V. Harper. *Hope Is Not a Method: What Business Leaders Can Learn from America's Army*. New York: Crown Business, 1997, p. 32.

Trusted Advisor, LLC, "Trust in Business: The Core Concepts," Trusted Advisor, LLC, https://trustedadvisor.com/articles/trust-in-business-the-core-concepts. Accessed December 18, 2018.

Wheatley, Margaret. *Leadership and the New Science: Discovering Order in a Chaotic World*. Oakland, CA: Berrett-Koehler Publishers, 2006, p. 89.

Wiseman, Liz, and Greg McKeown. "Managing Yourself: Bringing Out the Best in Your People." *Harvard Business Review*, May 2010, https://hbr.org/2010/05/managing-yourself-bringing-out-the-best-in-your-people.

Wicks, Robert J. *Bounce: Living the Resilient Life*. Oxford: Oxford University Press, 2009, pp. 33–34.

Wicks, Robert J. *Night Call: Embracing Compassion and Hope in a Troubled World*. Oxford: Oxford University Press, 2017, p. 24.

Yaeger, Don. "John Wooden's Legacy Is a How-To Guide for a Successful Life." *Success*, November 2, 2016, https://www.success.com/john-woodens-legacy-is-a-how-to-guide-for-a-successful-life/.

Zenger, Jack, and Joseph Folkman. "Nine Habits That Lead to Terrible Decisions." *Harvard Business Review*, September 1, 2014, https://hbr.org/2014/09/9-habits-that-lead-to-terrible-decisions.

CPSIA information can be obtained
at www.ICGtesting.com
Printed in the USA
LVHW070954280120
645047LV00017B/648